Lucille Mathurin Mair

THE CARIBBEAN BIOGRAPHY SERIES

The Caribbean Biography Series from the University of the West Indies Press celebrates and memorializes the architects of Caribbean culture. The series aims to introduce general readers to those individuals who have made sterling contributions to the region in their chosen field – literature, the arts, politics, sports – and are the shapers and bearers of Caribbean identity.

Other Titles in This Series

LUCILLE
MATHURIN
MAIR

Verene Shepherd

With research assistance by Stephanie Sewell

The University of the West Indies Press

Jamaica • Barbados • Trinidad and Tobago

The University of the West Indies Press
7A Gibraltar Hall Road, Mona
Kingston 7, Jamaica
www.uwipress.com

ISBN: 978-976-640-770-4 (cloth)
978-976-640-771-1 (paper)
978-976-640-772-8 (Kindle)
978-976-640-773-5 (ePub)

Cover photograph: Lucille Mathurin Mair in New Delhi, 1984.

Cover and book design by Robert Harris
Set in Whitman 11.5/15

Supported by the CHASE Fund, Jamaica

Printed in the United States of America

This book is dedicated to Lucille Mathurin Mair's children, Gail, David and Adrian Mathurin, without whom this biography would not have been possible, as well as to all the women whose lives were touched by her work and advocacy for gender justice.

CONTENTS

PREFACE

A s a history student at the University of the West Indies in the 1970s, it was inevitable that I would have been introduced to the work of Lucille Mathurin Mair, and later on in my life, I had the honour of meeting her. What struck me the first time I saw her in person as she gave a lecture on women and slavery at the Institute of Jamaica, however, was how impatient she was of historians who, in the face of archival evidence, pursued their political project of gender-blind history. As I developed in my career as a professional historian, I made sure that she could not count me among that derided group. Even though I met her a few more times between the late 1980s and when she died in 2009, I knew hardly anything about her background; and I would hazard a guess that neither did many Jamaicans, especially as she spent so much of her adult life outside the island. Now, through this biography, I have had a chance to help others to understand this phenomenal woman and the reasons for her philosophy of life and ideological positions.

Readers should imagine my delight, how mi glad bag buss, when I was asked by the University of the West Indies Press to participate in its Caribbean Biography Series by writing this biography. It is a signal honour for me to write about a woman who over the course of her life embraced the multiple roles of professional historian, wife, mother, mentor, diplomat, national and international civil servant, legislator, and women's rights activist; a woman who, through her scholar activism, successfully embodied and promoted the principles of justice and equality for women, especially women of the Global South; and someone recognized internationally for her activism in the struggle against all forms of discrimination and for the cause of peace and disarmament. Through interviews with her family, friends and colleagues, as well as through research of her own archives of speeches, lectures, letters, photographs and journal entries, the true measure of this marvellous woman, who served with such distinction at the national, regional and international levels, has been revealed and made accessible to a wider audience. This biography tells only part of a larger story that others will no doubt complete eventually.

Clearly, the decision to include Mair in the Caribbean Biography Series was a wise one, especially in light of her pivotal role in the journey to institutionalize gender studies at the University of the West Indies. Of course, she was far more than just an outstanding UWI woman. Among her voluminous boxes of papers, she has left a wealth of evidence of her contribution to the people of Cuba, Jamaica and St Lucia as well as to the United Nations and the academic and civil society communities in places where she delivered numerous lectures and speeches. She was a true citizen of the world, not just of the Caribbean, where she was born, grew up and lived most of her life. Mair's work allowed us to understand resistance and decolonizing politics and the role of the historian in shaping collective memory.

ONE

I saw my father for the first time through the haze of an October afternoon in London on the steps of the British Museum." Thus begins Lucille Walrond Mathurin Mair's description of meeting her biological father, the writer Eric Walrond, for the first time at twenty years old. The occasion was one of mixed emotions for the young Mair, who, in her own words, had endured "a childhood marked by huge and empty spaces longing to be filled".[1]

The long-anticipated meeting with the man who had fathered her was not a smooth affair. On the one hand, Mair was struck by Eric Walrond's youthful appearance and his sensitivity, and she respected his talents. On the other, she resented his refusal to explain why he had abandoned her, along with her mother and sisters. "He never explained away those years of silence; if there was remorse or guilt . . . he never voiced it if he ever found what he searched for across the Atlantic . . . and this was a problem for me." Happy as she was to have finally met her father, Mair knew instinctively that "nothing could fill the silent and empty spaces of that childhood longing".

Ironically, that fateful meeting with Eric Walrond had been arranged by the man who filled the role as father for her entire life, the Jamaican dentist Egbert "Eggie" Evans, her stepfather. Evans had raised and virtually adopted Mair and her sister Jean and Mair had developed a close bond with him. Enlisting the help of the outstanding Jamaican journalist and broadcaster Una Marson, who was an acquaintance of Eric Walrond, Evans had selflessly worked behind the scenes to bring father and daughter together for the first time.

Family sources shed little light on Mair's parents' ill-fated marriage and Walrond's absence from her life. What we do know is that Mair's mother, Edith Cadogan, first met Walrond sometime in 1917 in Colón, Panama, where Edith was visiting a relative. Eric was already well travelled. Born in British Guiana in 1898, he moved with his mother, Ruth, and his siblings to her native Barbados in 1906, after his Guyanese father, William, all but abandoned them when he left for Panama. In 1910, his destitute wife took the children to Panama in search of her errant husband. Eric was educated in Panama and worked for the Panama *Star and Herald* as a journalist, a profession he continued to practise when he left Panama for New York City in 1918.

He settled first in Brooklyn with his aunt and uncle (Julia and Charles Nicholls), where Edith, by then a stenographer, was also living. The two married on 26 November 1920 at Eric's home in Manhattan.[2] It is still unclear if they left Panama together or if Edith joined him later after she returned to Jamaica from that trip. The marriage did not last long: after three years the couple separated, with Edith returning home to Jamaica. By then the union had produced two girls, Jean and Dorothy, with Lucille on the way. We know that a pregnant Edith arrived in Kingston in 1924 with her two daughters and chose to raise them both there. It is likely that they stayed with her sister Lil and her husband, Jim Williamson, a renowned jeweller and businessman. Lucille was born in Kingston at the Victoria Jubilee Hospital on 21 June 1924. We are unsure how Edith supported herself and her children, but Mair's eldest child and only daughter, Gail, and niece Jeanette Campbell recall hearing rumours that their grandmother worked in a salon in the Cross Roads area of Kingston, perhaps before marrying Evans in 1934, following her divorce from Walrond.

The little we know of Mair's parents, including her stepfather, and her relationship with them is to be found in a journal she kept. In it, Mair had little to say about her mother, her siblings and other family members, but she did record that she was brought up by "an evangelical, strong-willed mother whose acid tongue was curiously reticent on the subject of her first husband". Family members who have memories of Edith said that she was "high brown" and a snob who looked down on working-class black people, especially her domestic workers; and even though she had married black men, discouraged her daughters and granddaughters from doing the same. It is possible that she made an exception for professional black men. Oral history indicates that Edith was a descendant of Barbadian whites who had emigrated to Jamaica in search of land, eventually settling in an area known as Cadogan Hill in the parish of Hanover in the western end of the island.

Mair had much more to say about her father. Journal entries

include an unfinished piece called "Memories of a Father Lost and Found", suggesting that she may have been drafting her memoirs, and devoted space to Eric Walrond based on the space reserved for him in her journal. Even with the writing, rewriting and crossing out, there is firm evidence of her feelings towards him. She expressed disappointment at the fact that her biological father had abandoned her mother and sisters and neglected his paternal role without explanation. Others have subsequently tried to offer a reason for his behaviour, linking it to his inability to support his family in New York and to his bouts of depression and feelings of displacement from living in racist societies.[3] If he is talking about Edith in a story called "Cynthia Goes to the Prom", then an additional reason could be that she never shared his passion for pan-Africanism and black consciousness.[4]

Mair was clearly emotionally wounded by her father's abandonment, but her stepfather became an excellent surrogate father to her and her sister Jean. Mair gives him the credit for encouraging her and putting her through university. (The other sister, Dorothy, was eventually placed with a family member in Washington, DC, and remained in the United States.) Mair described Evans in her journal as "a supremely self-confident spirit, who assumed that anyone close to him was nothing less than perfect". Evans had graduated from Howard University in 1916 and returned home to establish a successful dental practice on Duke Street in Kingston.

Mair began her formal education at Morris Knibb Preparatory School before entering Wolmer's High School for Girls, both in Kingston. It was at Wolmer's that headmistress Evelyn

Skempton identified young Mair as an exceptional student, and encouraged her to pursue higher studies. She was among six students from her school in her generation who sat both the Senior Cambridge Examinations and the Higher Schools Certificate – a privilege previously reserved only for boys. Mrs Skempton became one of the principal driving forces behind Mair's acceptance and eventual departure to pursue a university degree in London. Mair also spoke fondly of Minnie Forbes, her history teacher, "a classic Victorian spinster", who taught her to be confident, and inspired in her a love for the subject of history.[5] In her own words, "I had no question in my mind that History was going to be my subject." In 1990, at a prize-giving ceremony at her alma mater, she paid tribute to Minnie Forbes by declaring: "the decision to make a career in history . . . had a lot to do with the person who really introduced me to history and who generously communicated to me her own passionate interest in the subject. . . . Miss Minnie [Forbes] shared with me her affection and her concern for me as a young girl growing up trying to understand life, trying to decide what to make of the future."

Mair likely also revered Miss Anna Hollar, who taught her English: as she recorded it, there were very few people of colour at Wolmer's Girls and for several years, she had never been taught by someone of her own complexion. At the ceremony in 1990, she told the girls that in her days "the very content of our syllabuses at that time, geography, history, literature, had little or nothing to do with the Caribbean in which I lived", an experience not dissimilar to the one described in Olive Senior's poem "Colonial Girls School".

Upon completing her secondary education, Mair taught for some years at Wolmer's and also at Excelsior High School. She was not able to begin undergraduate studies immediately after completing her secondary education, as World War II had broken out by then, severely restricting travel across the Atlantic.

Her adolescent years during the 1930s and 1940s were of paramount importance in shaping her before she left for university. Not only was she a product of, and influenced by, the labour protests and the accompanying political ferment they generated in Jamaica and the wider Caribbean, but she was also affected by the repercussions of the two world wars. She was known to participate in political and social discussions at her stepfather's house at 4 Argyle Road in Kingston at a time when colonies in the British Caribbean were exposed to harsh living conditions and political anxiety. She participated in discussions about the People's National Party (PNP) and Norman Manley, and about nationalism, a phenomenon that had gripped many countries around the world and had even bred revolutions in some. She recalled sitting in on Sunday afternoon sessions at Henry and Greta Fowler's home. Henry Fowler was one of the early members of the PNP and supported the lobby for Jamaica's independence from Britain.[6]

The Fowlers also founded the Little Theatre Movement, which gave birth to the annual pantomime as well as other productions. Mair was one of the first black women to be featured in one of these pantomimes, playing the princess in the 1943 *Soliday and the Wicked Bird*. She was also the narrator in a play pre-recorded in August 1948, entitled *The Mixed Heritage*, which covered the period of Spanish invasion and colonization and the reasons for their brand of colonialism.

Mair's passion for theatre continued long into her adult years. Clark Cousins, son of Irena Cousins, a long-time friend and colleague of Mair's, fondly remembers attending many a pantomime as well as plays at the Philip Sherlock Centre for the Creative Arts, then known as the Creative Arts Centre, on the Mona campus of the University of the West Indies (UWI), and seeing Mair accompanied by her youngest son Adrian. He recalls being "'handcuffed' as escort for both Aunt Lucille and mum [Irena Cousins] to go to plays. . . . They enjoyed the tête à tête during intermissions . . . and talking to all the admiring gentlemen."[7]

The Fowlers also established the Jamaica Theatre School, later renamed the School of Drama under the Cultural Training Centre, now the Edna Manley College for the Visual and Performing Arts. Mair was a member of this institution, as well as of the Jamaica School of Art. While she was a teenager, she was also involved in the Young Women's Christian Association and its leadership-development workshops.

Once World War II was over, Mair lost no time in travelling to London to begin her university studies, enrolling at University College London to read for a bachelor of arts degree. She graduated with honours in history in 1948. Mair also had an interest in economics and confessed her regret at not being able to attend lectures by Harold Laski, renowned political theorist, economist and anti-colonialist, at the London School of Economics.[8] Nevertheless, she and other Caribbean students were fortunate to have had an opportunity to learn from the brilliant Caribbean economist and future Nobel Laureate Sir W. Arthur Lewis, then lecturer at the London School of Economics.

At university, Mair was an active member (and for a time, secretary) of the West Indian Students' Union. She shared ideas and perspectives with other great thinkers, such as Elsa Goveia (first professor of history at the University College of the West Indies), Errol Barrow (first prime minister of Barbados), Leslie Robinson (first principal of the Mona campus of the UWI), Forbes Burnham (first prime minister of Guyana) and Michael Manley (fourth prime minister of Jamaica). She was also influenced by the ideologies of Eric Williams (first prime minister of Trinidad and Tobago), who by then had published his Oxford thesis, *Capitalism and Slavery*. This was a period of heightened cultural and regional awareness, when, being the brightest and the best from their respective countries, these influencers all held strong views about social issues related to identity, colonialism and independence of the Caribbean region. They were all to become leaders, pioneers and great thinkers, all passionate and prepared to return home to fight against injustice, discrimination and oppression of the poor and vulnerable, which was institutionalized under the colonial regimes in their respective countries.

Her friend Sonia Mills explains: "Lucille Mair came from an era that was very anti-colonial and nationalistic, which means she had very strong opinions on nationalism and independence; and she was not shy about making her positions heard or felt. It was a time in the world when the so-called Third World was very prominent in discussions on the new international order at the level of the United Nations. Diplomats from the 'Third

World' also hoped to change the UN and the world."[9] Some of Mair's Caribbean counterparts embarked on this mission through politics; Mair, however, chose academia to demonstrate the power of the politics of memory.

It was while studying in London that Mair met the love of her life, Guy Mathurin, who had won the 1942 St Lucia Island Scholarship and was studying for the Bar in London.[10] The two were married in a private ceremony, after which Mathurin returned to St Lucia and opened the first local professional law firm in the island with attorney Garnet Gordon, called Gordon, Salles-Miquelle, Mathurin and Co. Mair remained in London for another year studying for her teacher's diploma, specializing in English history, at the University of London. During this time, she shared a flat with Michael Manley and his first wife, Jacqueline Ramellard.

Mair arrived in St Lucia in 1949 and taught briefly at St Joseph's Convent School in Castries, the capital, where she was the first person ever to teach a course in West Indian history. She opened the eyes of these students to the harsh experiences endured by their ancestors during the transatlantic trade in enslaved Africans and during the period of enslavement, and taught of the resilience and strength of enslaved females and their roles in resistance movements. Unfortunately, her history lessons did not last long, as the school "scrubbed" the course as it was deemed too "ideologically open".[11] Also noteworthy is that she was only the second teacher at St Joseph's who was not a nun, as well as the first pregnant woman to teach there. She played a role similar to Headmistress Skempton at Wolmer's by encouraging her students to pursue university studies. Her efforts were not in vain, as in 1955, an Island Scholarship was won for the first time by a female student, Daphne Monplaisir, whom Mair had taught and tutored at St Joseph's. There, she earned the nickname "Ma Matts", which remained with her for several years. While in St Lucia, Mair also worked in the Extra-Mural Unit for the Windwards at the University College of the West Indies, in Castries, where many future professionals and businesswomen were to come under her influence. Mair's students in St Lucia remember her as a brilliant teacher, precise in her speech and generous with her time, recalling that "no one ever failed the subjects taught by Mathurin Mair in these external exams".[12]

The Mathurins led a full social and professional life in St Lucia. Mair made friends with St Lucian poet and playwright Derek Walcott, in whose first wedding she participated as matron of honour for the bride. The Mathurins were members of the St Lucia Historical Society, and Mair was a founding member of the St Lucia Women's Association, formed on 21 July 1953. The couple's three children – Gail, David and Adrian – were born in St Lucia.

In the midst of this apparently happy and fulfilling life, tragedy struck on 27 July 1957, when Guy Mathurin was involved in a motor vehicle accident and succumbed to his injuries. Out of this loss, Mair's career at the University College of the West Indies began when Sir Philip Sherlock invited her to come to the Mona campus in Jamaica and start a new life. She was to make good use of her relocation, pursuing a doctorate in history, becoming involved in national politics and going on to become a star on the international stage, especially at the United Nations.

TWO

Guy Mathurin's sudden and untimely death left a gaping hole in Mair's life. In the eight years of their marriage, she had become fully integrated into St Lucian society, both through her individual career pursuits and interests and those she shared with her husband. While his passing had not left her penniless or helpless, her life had been anchored to his. Going it alone meant starting over again with three young children and no guarantee of financial stability. So when the opportunity came to return home to Jamaica to take up the post of warden of the newly established Mary Seacole Hall, the first all-female hall of residence on the Mona campus of the University College of the West Indies, Mair readily accepted. Her appointment officially began on 1 September 1957, although the hall was not actually opened for accommodation until 1958.

In many respects, Mair was the ideal person to assume responsibility for the guidance and welfare of impressionable student residents, many away from home for the first time, some from outside of Jamaica. Her experiences in St Lucia as teacher and mentor at St Joseph's and her work with women at the Extra-Mural Centre were preparation for the challenging task ahead. The transition was not an easy one for Mair, who expressed feelings of vulnerability to her friends as she adjusted to the loss of her husband, life in Jamaica and the presence of hundreds of students. As Velma Pollard, one of Mair's first charges at Seacole and later a professor at UWI, later observed: "Here was a woman, grieving, but not obviously so; trying to manage a job and three small children in a new Hall, with a large number of young women."[3] Before long, however, Mair threw off all her anxieties and began to impose her own brand of discipline and leadership style on the running of the hall.

Her relationship with her charges often went beyond the arm's-length warden-student relationship, as she became counsellor and surrogate mother to several. However, this was never at the expense of maintaining a strict disciplinary regime, including a rigidly enforced 10:00 p.m. curfew and a rule of no male visitors being allowed past the porter's lodge. Mair's daughter, Gail, recalls some of her male fellow students discussing confrontations with her mother as they attempted to sneak out of the hall. Musician Marjorie Whylie fondly recalls her own attempts at sneaking in and out of the residence through a hole in the metal gate.[14] Other students devised even more creative means of passive resistance against the tight regimen of the hall, such as wearing short nighties under the gowns worn at formal dinners, and sneaking through the back fence to congregate at the Students' Union for an "S.T." (as small talk or otherwise was known).

Former prime minister of Jamaica P.J. Patterson, who was the student chairman of the neighbouring all-male Chancellor Hall during Mair's tenure as warden of Seacole, tells the story that she would often appear seemingly out of nowhere shortly after 10:00 p.m. to welcome the return of her charges and to thank their escorts for seeing them safely home.

Mair presided over formal hall dinners complete with china, starched napkins and silverware, at which the young women were required to dress for dinner and act as hostesses for guests who would often come to entertain or give a talk to the students. For each dinner, a group of students was identified to be responsible for meeting and greeting the guests and accompanying them at the dinner. The women were encouraged to listen and engage their guests in discussion on the topic for that evening's address.

Mair's aim was to provide the young women of Seacole Hall with an education that transcended day-to-day learning in the classroom by exposing them to the social graces and additional intellectual stimulation through an awareness of current affairs. She would also invite some of the students to tea at her home, which was in the precincts of the hall, where the conversation included discussion of social issues. This was her way of ensuring that the students acquired confidence and could hold their own in a variety of social settings and express opinions without fear.

In spite of the strict code of conduct that Mair imposed on her charges and the restrictive rules by which she administered Seacole Hall, she was well loved by the generations of women who lived in residence over the almost two decades of her tenure. Notwithstanding the designation "Chastity Hall" and the title of a carnival tune, "Beware of the Mair", with which she was associated, she is remembered fondly by students who came under her influence. Former UN ambassador for Jamaica Patricia Durrant thought she "provided a model of all that an educated woman could and should be. She combined grace, charm, wit and intellect, independent-mindedness and self-confidence with a brilliant mind."[5] Velma Pollard also recalled her elegance, noting that Mair was always appropriately dressed, with a stylish simplicity, and each of her outfits was paired with a short heel or a beautiful pair of sandals. It is said that even young male students were swept away by her physical appearance, grace and fashion. She was tall and poised, and would always turn heads, without trying to do so.

The warden's home at Seacole was like a home away from home for many of the students who interacted with Mair's children and other "campus babies". It was as if the female residents under her charge were an extension of her own family as her children grew into their teens and themselves became part of the Seacole family. In considering her dual roles as warden and full-time single mother to her own three children, David Mathurin, her middle child, says that she did a wonderful job at finding a balance and taking care of them all. School holidays were family affairs often spent in rural Jamaica as well as in urban and peri-urban communities such as Bull Bay in St Andrew, Mullion Cove in Westmoreland and Cacoon in Hanover where some of their relatives resided. The children frequently visited their maternal grandparents at their home on Argyle Road in Kingston before they both died within a short time of each other. Edith Cadogan-Evans died after a long battle with Alzheimer's, a disease that was also to afflict one of Mair's sisters and lead to Mair's own demise many years later.

Outside of life in Seacole Hall, Mair was heavily involved in the intense debates that were a feature of campus life in the 1960s and early years of the 1970s. The campus was a melting pot not only of Caribbean people, but also of Caribbean culture and intellectual thought. Questions of independence and colonization carried over from the West Indian Students' Union in London were revived on the university campus, as did discussions on regional integration and efforts to collaborate more profoundly as a region. Mair crossed paths with several women and men who would later become icons of the Caribbean, among them C.L.R. James, Lloyd Best, Alister McIntyre and Peggy Antrobus, who became a leading figure in the feminist movement.

Mair was as intolerant of racism as she was of sexism. Apart from her high school experience, perhaps the other issue that had a profound influence on her was the treatment of Walter Rodney, a Guyanese lecturer at UWI, by the Jamaican government. Rodney was a noted historian and political activist and a significant figure in the Black Power movement in the Caribbean. The Jamaica Labour Party government under Prime Minister Hugh Shearer saw him as subversive, declared him persona non grata in October 1968 and exiled him from Jamaica.

The UWI student body caught wind of the government's decision and planned a demonstration in support of Rodney. The students were to wear red gowns on the march to distinguish them from non-student protesters, but this effort proved futile, as many other demonstrators joined the march clothed in red tunics, overalls and other coloured apparel, protesting high prices and general poor quality of life. The march became violent: tear gas was thrown, cars were burned and several people were injured.

Among those caught in the chaos of the march was Gail Mathurin, who had to call her mother to pick her up, as she was stranded and afraid in downtown Kingston. By some miracle, Mair was able to drive to her location and bring her back to safety. Rodney's pregnant wife, Patricia, also participated in the march, with her neighbour sustaining leg injuries after being hit and burned by a gas canister, and she herself feeling ill after having walked back to campus. It was none other than Mair who opened her doors to Patricia to stay at her home for a week to ensure that she could receive adequate medical attention. She recalls Mair being gracious and welcoming. As the ban was never lifted, Patricia eventually left Jamaica with her child to join her husband in London.

Although Mair supported Rodney and his philosophy and sympathized with the students' actions, she did not join the street protests. She believed that protests would not be an effective measure for spreading black consciousness in Jamaica and that the movement would eventually fizzle out without support from the then government. She preferred a more diplomatic approach that focused on targeted radio interviews and broadcasts and structured meetings. She believed the old saying "pressure buss pipe", confident that continued pressure would yield more beneficial results than strikes. She feared that the peaceful protests would be infiltrated by violence, which would ultimately dissuade sympathizers and some supporters of the movement – not to mention the government. Unfortunately, she was right.

In 1969, Mair published a seminal article entitled "The Student and the University's Civilising Role" for a special issue of *Caribbean Quarterly* marking the retirement of Sir Philip Sherlock and the twentieth anniversary of the university,[16] It is worth quoting at length for her rare insight into what life was like in those heady years of the 1960s:

> The residential pattern of the University gave this small group maximum opportunity for intense, sustained and furiously competitive interaction.... The novelty of West Indianism had been, from the very beginning, an important fact at Mona. But students carried their regional awareness easily; it was the delighted, spontaneous recognition of kinship, reflected in light-hearted inter-island exchange of "picong". A few postured about it, the student leader, for example, who with a special emphasis, often announced himself as a "West Indian who happened to be born in Jamaica". But no trauma here; the society was largely indifferent; Carnival, calypso, steel band and roti found ready homes on campus. (11)

Commenting on the intellectual ferment of the period, she continued:

> Another strenuous intellectual exercise, outside of the curriculum, marked this period. This was the series of weekly open lectures by distinguished scholars which started in 1958, and which dealt with a range of topics including philosophy, law, Africa, literature, the idea of a University, etc., and ended abruptly in 1960 when a car accident prevented Mr. C.L.R. James from completing his course of talks. Large numbers of staff and students regularly attended and took part in the discussions which followed in the

Common Rooms of Halls and in the homes of staff members. It was the last campus-wide conversation of any value between staff and students. After that the pattern crystallised that a few staff spoke to a few students; for the rest, never the twain did meet. It was also the last probing attempt of students to define a University in abstract terms, and to codify the new West Indian spirit. (13)

In the same article she provides a comparison of life on the Mona campus in the early days of the UWI, then the University College of the West Indies, in the 1950s and at the point of publication in 1969. Noteworthy is her account of how student life, student and staff interaction and interactions between students and the rest of the population had evolved throughout her tenure at the university and the kinds of expectations that society had of its graduates:

There is a parallel here with the Jamaican view of the traveller, explored with shrewdness by that wise analyst of local neurosis, Louise Bennett. Her Mary's Dry Foot Bwoy is pulled up sharply for the affected accent he brings back with him from abroad, and the community mounts a campaign of ridicule to bring him back into line. But just as real is the disappointment with the son who returns unchanged from his American stay – "and you come back not a piece betta dan how yuh did goh wey? . . . not even lickle language bwoy? not even lickle twang?" To remain the same is equally unforgiveable. What Jamaican or West Indian society seems to want of its student, is the best of both worlds, "improvement" without irritation. The student may enjoy a few years of slovenliness and any number of mild flirtations with the current -isms, so long as he returns to the fold with his shoes polished, his hair combed, and his visible sign of improvement, his degree, safely under his belt. (8)

Mair's article gives credit to the sheer brilliance of the students at the university, noting that they were historically the "pick of the intellectual crop" (9), which meant that it was no surprise that the campus became a breeding ground for intellectual discussions, debates, and even demonstrations among students and staff alike, and became the place of activists, political scientists, playwrights and historians. She looked at the transitions in discussions among staff and students in different eras, going from lecture halls, to halls of residence, to the student union, eventually working their way into various forms of media. Current UWI students would possibly know of the *Pelican*, which was recently been resurrected in the form of the *Pelican Magazine* for the sixtieth anniversary of the university, and possibly the *Pelican Bit*, but how many have heard of the other short-lived periodicals, such as *Impact*, *Rising Star* and *Scope?*

Throughout that period, several national and regional-level issues would emerge to occupy the minds and time of students, from the rise and fall of the West Indies Federation, to the entrance into the "first phase of nervous nationalism" (17), to Jamaica's changing political climate, decisions made by the government and implications for the Mona campus. She described the campus of her time as a creative hub, attracting, honing and displaying talents in all forms of arts and in sports, including showcasing the likes of her later friends, counterparts and students. She noted especially the success of these students in the performing arts and the contrasting interests of students on the campus:

> Talent abounded; this was the era of Walcott, the poet, painter, dramatist, and sometime student; and the medical undergrad-

uate who was also athlete, debater, orator, photographer, hor-
ticulturist, was not entirely unique. The residential pattern of
the University gave this small group maximum opportunity for
intense, sustained and furiously competitive interaction. As a
result, individuals pursued wide-ranging extra-curricular activi-
ties with outstanding success, in the music room and the common
room, on the sports field and on the stage. . . .

But on the whole, the arts, rather than the politics of Federation, seemed the stronger interest, and inspired the University
Players to peak of brilliance not since equalled, with their 1956
production of Walcott's *Sea at Dauphin*, the outstanding piece of
the Jamaica Drama Festival that year which walked off with the
honours in acting, production and playwriting. (9, 11)

UWI students in the 2000s would have merely heard stories of the protests and heightened student activism of former
UWI graduates. They would not have, like Mair, witnessed the
mobilization of students against the university and national
authorities in a series of protests (and other forms of demonstration) on matters such as the Rodney protests in 1968 and the
rising Black Power movement, the 1964 strike at the Jamaica
Broadcasting Corporation, the government security policy,
Rhodesia, apartheid and the Sharpeville massacre, which sent
students and members of staff on "a solemn march through
the streets of Kingston, and down to the Victoria Pier, where
they held a mass meeting to protest Apartheid inhumanity.
The demonstration touched on no local issues, and implied no
sharp divisions within the campus structure: it was a unique
and impressive display of University unity and idealism, which
earned the respect and approval of the Jamaican public and
press" (13–14, 18).

One celebrated event in 1960 had to do with the wards under Mair's careful watch whose demonstration in front of the university's chancellor, HRH Princess Alice, and the Princess Royal, earned them maximum press coverage and some approbation. Mary Seacole women were tired of dining at Irvine Hall, having no dining room of their own. Recalling it, Mair wrote. "By this act the undergraduate society suddenly emancipated itself." It was described as "a determined, silent and dignified" affair. "It had its critics, those who deplored the impropriety of students demonstrating before two members of the Royal Family: and those who felt it a waste that all that dignity, determination etc., had not been put to a bigger and a better cause" (13).

In the *Caribbean Quarterly* article, Mair also mentioned the difficulty that the university had in connecting to the students and the decreasing interaction between student and staff, perhaps because of the shift in location for discussion to a focus on hall life, rather than the Senior Common Room and the Students' Union as it once was. She noted: "The falling levels of student participation and performance in the 60's reflect the absence of an efficient structure. Some groups, it is true, notably the religious societies, continue steadily to appeal. And the University has never failed in any year to produce outstanding persons in every field, from music to athletics to debating; it is the corporate achievement that has been lacking" (15).

The collapse of the West Indies Federation plunged the UWI into a new era, where a decade-long debate and rapport between student and lecturer dissolved, leaving way for the emergence of student activism. But even that activism rapidly decreased over the years, to the extent that, Mair concluded, "A curious state of limbo hangs over Mona today. Clearly it cannot last. It may be that there is no turning back to the culture of the Common Room as the campus once knew it; the excursion into the streets of the city carry very painful, ineradicable memories of stinging teargas, and the thud of police batons. Students can always turn to their textbooks and this may well be where society is happiest to see them buried" (18).

❧

The focus so far has been on Mair's seventeen-year tenure as warden of Mary Seacole Hall and a description of the impact she had on the students who came under her influence. But her life was not one-dimensional: between 1963 and 1965 she also acted as the vice chancellor's special assistant on university development and fundraising, which today would be a job for two people at the level of a pro-vice chancellor. And in 1970 she was asked to be the vice chancellor's representative to the United Kingdom to administer the Princess Alice University Appeal. Beyond these administrative duties, Mair's Seacole years were characterized by two important milestones, one of which would define the trajectory of her life and career. In the early 1960s she registered as a PhD student in the Department of History. Elsa Goveia agreed to supervise her. By that time, they were already great friends, having first met as students in London. Mair would later describe Goveia as "my teacher, my friend and my contemporary". Of the decision to read for the doctorate, she is quoted as saying, "I recall discussing this with Elsa and she encouraged me. Without that support and inspiration I would not have dug into the past. It took me many years but it was so worthwhile and I was facilitated in the process" ("Sterling Mark Made by Mair", *Sunday Sun*, 7 July 1996, 2a). It is clear that Goveia's impact on Mair was monumental: "I do not hesitate to call her an ancestor because of the impact of her work on the literary heritage of the Caribbean."[17]

The result of Mair's work was the groundbreaking thesis "A Historical Study of Women in Jamaica, 1655–1844". She was the first person known to have written a full-length doctoral thesis entirely based on Caribbean women. The thesis became one of the most sought-after works, as writers and academics were stunned at the magnitude of research she had done, and the prospect of what was left to be done in this uncharted territory. She was a first in many regards and was no doubt the object of an "incurable envy" by some in her community. This she overcame, according to Rex Nettleford, with "a stubborn determination to remain focused on what she thought was necessary, as well as by a dignified detachment, a well cultivated appearance of invincibility and resilience and unflappable charming engagement with all that would conspire to blur her vision".[18]

It was at the University College of the West Indies that Mair's passion for women's issues developed, as the more she interacted with the women on hall, the greater her belief in the infinite possibilities of women. Her choice of subject for her research and final thesis paved the way for an emerging movement in women's studies and focus on the role of women in West Indian history.

The other significant milestone of these Seacole years was a second marriage, to Ian Mair, a family friend and colleague of her deceased husband. Ian was an English architect living in Antigua at the time. He had been a friend to Mair while she was mourning the loss of her first husband and they grew closer as time passed. The marriage took place on 15 September 1962, at the University Chapel, leaving the women in Seacole awestruck by the romance of their warden and the wedding itself. Sadly, the two found the relationship unsustainable after a few years of travelling back and forth between Antigua and Jamaica. Ian had his heart set on his wife and her youngest child, Adrian, moving to Antigua, but she was against this idea, given her commitment to the task of firmly establishing Mary Seacole Hall and the completion of her doctoral studies. She was also reluctant to once again uproot her children, who knew little of Ian and did not get very involved in the relationship between their mother and their stepfather. They divorced and she moved on.

Mair did her best to balance her responsibilities as mother alongside her duties as warden, research student and part-time lecturer. Although at times she had to leave her children at home in the company of friends or staff at Mary Seacole Hall, they did accompany her on a couple of research trips to London in 1964 and 1970.

Mair's mother, Edith, accompanied her on one such trip and Mair took the opportunity to bring her parents together in London, where Walrond had settled many years before. The children met their biological grandfather for the first time, but they were indifferent to this tall, handsome man and can recall no visible signs of bitterness, anger or sadness. For Mair, however, the encounter with Walrond was a memorable one and as in her first meeting, she experienced conflicted emotions. She later wrote in her journal, "It was too late for him to re-enter the home he had left behind . . . too late for him to regain a lost family. . . . He knew this and accepted it like the man he was." By then "he was ill, less vigorous; and we tried to know each other". He died two years later, in 1966.

Mair took care not to spoil her children and did not believe in using her position or friendships with influential people to obtain privileges for them. Her older son, David, pursued an undergraduate degree between 1969 and 1973 in management and economics at Yale University and a doctorate at the University of Rochester, later going to work with the Caribbean Development Bank in Barbados. When Mair later relocated to New York to assume the post of Jamaica's deputy permanent representative to the United Nations, mother and son managed to maintain a close relationship. Adrian also spent time with her while a college student in New York before relocating to St Lucia. Gail, by the 1980s, had also begun her career as a diplomat with the Ministry of Foreign Affairs in Jamaica.

Perhaps the only discordant note in Mair's tenure as warden of Seacole Hall was a long-running dialogue with the university administration over having her post as warden upgraded, with an accompanying salary increase. She had been warden for eight and a half years when in 1966 she first requested a promotion to a higher grade. Alas, she was advised that the post carried no provision for promotion beyond the equivalent salary scale of lecturer or assistant registrar. Undaunted, she made another request in 1973 and, in an exchange of correspondence with both the vice chancellor and the university registrar, expressed her disappointment at her situation not being addressed, pointing out that she had been held at the same pay grade for fifteen years, and observed that no other category of staff had been so penalized. She requested that her case be favourably considered in the interest of equity. Her persistence eventually led the university to agree in 1973 to revise the ordinance for the promotion of wardens on the basis of administrative ability, contribution to university life and public service. Mair qualified on all three counts and in January 1974 was offered a promotion to the grade of senior lecturer for an indefinite tenure "on the grounds of long service". Her salary was also increased above the band paid only to heads of department and readers.

This episode, seen through the correspondence with the university administration, displayed a bold, assertive, resolute and persistent Mair, who stood up for what she believed in, especially in a case of injustice and inequality, but always in a respectful and non-confrontational manner. Her initial motivation might have been to plead for an improvement in her personal status, but her advocacy led to the university's changing its ordinance to benefit all wardens. Ironically, having struggled for so long to achieve this benefit, she was never to enjoy it, as in that same year, 1974, she was seconded with no pay for a period of two years to take up the post of director of the Agency for Public Information, during the first Michael Manley administration.

Mair never returned to her substantive post as warden of Mary Seacole Hall, as by 1975 she had been recruited to the diplomatic service as Jamaica's deputy permanent representative to the United Nations in New York. When her request for an extension of the two-year secondment was turned down by the university, she officially resigned from the institution on 31 July 1976. She closed her brief letter of resignation by saying: "I shall have the warmest memories of my years at Mona and I will be happy to continue to be of service in any way I can."

Mair always reflected positively about the UWI and her years at Mary Seacole Hall. In a lecture she gave at Medgar Evers College in 1992, she said, "During those years . . . I worked and lived with hundreds of the brightest, energetic, cantankerous, creative and most wonderful young people to be found anywhere in the world. . . . The UWI continues to be a most important Caribbean institution, providing a collective will and capability to address the regional challenges which face us and continues to do this with energy and determination despite formidable odds."

Reflecting further on her life at Mary Seacole, in her acceptance speech at the CARICOM Triennial Awards in 1996, she noted that "I had the children and I had a heck of a time keeping them out of the students' rooms. It was a good time in my life. I had a great deal of responsibilities and enjoyed every minute of it." Indeed, the Mary Seacole years influenced Mair's career trajectory: she was also to affirm that "this is how my interest in the whole subject of women, their condition past and present developed".[19]

THREE

It would not be an exaggeration to say that Mair was first and foremost a historian, especially after 1974, when she was armed with a PhD in history from the UWI. The knowledge gained from the process of researching and writing that pioneering thesis, as well as the revelations from her research and her keen insight into the ways in which contemporary societies were affected by the past, were later to inform her actions, writings and speeches. In our introduction to the book version of Mair's thesis, my co-editor and I wrote,

> She considered her project a first step in the morning. Having opened the door, she was not prepared to follow the well-known markers along the old road. She crossed over to the other side, turned her face in the opposite direction, and journeyed off in search of the woman lost to Caribbean history; the woman, she knew intuitively, was not hidden from history nor lost in it. Rather she was hidden by history.[20]

Regardless of the posts Mair held, she used historical knowledge to inform and teach. History made her an advocate for women's rights, gender justice and equality in the age of globalization. She is counted among that band of UWI graduates who were scholar activists and who climbed over the walls of academia to demonstrate the transformative power of history education to a people seeking a more liberating narrative of self. The activism of pioneers like Mair and Rodney resides in the historical memory of the UWI. In "The Role of the Historian in the Developing West Indies", Rodney argued persuasively that "it is one of the tasks of the historian of the West Indies to approach the society in a different manner and to lay emphasis on precisely what was going on in the region. This would certainly lead to the presentation of new heroes with whom the West Indian people would identify themselves – an important psychological necessity." He thought that the UWI should "assume responsibility for popularizing such knowledge".[21] This is what Mair did in "A Historical Study of Women in Jamaica, 1655–1844".

In a letter to the *Feminist Press* (5 June 1985), Mair described the work as "the first and to date the only comprehensive historical treatment of this topic". She explained that it dealt with the impact of colonialism, racism and sexism on white, black and coloured women in Jamaican slave society. It begins with "the arrivants",[22] then turns to the establishment of creole society, followed by developments set in the post-slavery period. Each section focuses on the different experiences of women based on their race (white, black and mixed race) and class (elite, indentured and poor white; free black and mixed; and unfree black and mixed).

When Mair's thesis was published many years later,[23] it was well reviewed. One reviewer wrote, "The power of this comparative gendered analysis was absolutely groundbreaking in Caribbean history. It's not just that women are at the center, but also that their recorded lives and experiences are thereby made critical to understanding the history of Jamaican society and culture. Here commonalities among women . . . are discussed and examined with extraordinary care and finesse."[24]

Indeed, the field of women's history was heavily influenced by Mair's work. Her writings and published output were by no means limited to her converted thesis. While that book was unquestionably her magnum opus, over her career she wrote and had published numerous articles, opinion pieces and lectures as she continued to delve deeper into the theme of women under the slavery regime in Jamaica, resistance to systems of domination, feminism and women's activism.

A small illustrated book derived from the thesis was published in 1975 and remains popular today: *The Rebel Woman in the British West Indies during Slavery.*[25] In it, Mair focuses on the African roots of enslaved women's agency, and insists that they carried their fighting spirit especially from that area called the Gold Coast (modern-day Ghana). She outlines the forms of agency including day-to-day acts of non-cooperation, marronage, guerrilla warfare and armed revolt. Above all, she discusses the rationale for enslaved women's activism – ending slavery. *Rebel Woman* addresses the common yet false belief that women took a passive stance to enslavement. Rather, with examples from the life of Queen Nanny, or Nana, of the Windward Maroons in Jamaica, Mair demonstrates the many ways in which women contributed to the liberation movement, thereby deconstructing the myths of woman as the submissive sex, and addressing the absence of women in early historical documentation of the period of enslavement. Gender distinctions were not observed in categories of work; and women were not exempted from harsh punishments that inevitably followed in the wake of resistance, as Mair states:

> Africans who were brought as [enslaved people] to the New World did not accept their condition meekly. They employed a variety of methods to express their resentment of the institution of slavery, and of the white masters who enslaved them. They employed quiet, subtle, almost negative methods of protest which today might be termed civil disobedience; for example, they pretended to be ill, and so avoided work. On the other hand, they sometimes went to the positive, violent extreme of armed rebellion. . . .
>
> It is not so well established that women, who are often regarded as the submissive sex, also took an important part in forms of protest against slavery. [Enslaved women] adopted some of the same techniques as men to defy the system: they frequently ran away from the plantation, on their own, or in mixed groups: and in addition they resisted in ways which were peculiar to them as women: for example they could, and did use periods of childbearing to do the minimum of work, and to extract the maximum of concessions from their masters.[26]

Mair also contributed chapters to edited collections in which she addressed the invisibility and absence of women in European documentation of New World plantations; the strategies used by Europeans to subordinate women and diminish their contributions to economic viability; and women's reproductive rights that were quashed by a system that prioritized production over reproduction. It is remarkable how, decades later, her arguments remain profoundly relevant: "Reproductive rights occupy a central place among women's search for justice and claims to self-determination. . . . Reproductive rights, in fact, are the least negotiable items on women's agenda of rights."[27]

She wrote opinion pieces for local and international newspapers, including one critiquing the story of Annie Palmer, the alleged White Witch of Rose Hall,[28] a famous Jamaican tale: "Was Annie's unorthodoxy then a frantic bid for recognition as person, not plaything?" she asked in her *Gleaner* article. "In daring to do what her menfolk had always done, did she become a victim of masculine outrage? . . . There is another important practical side to this legend; when the male power structure cannot beat the feminists, it commercializes them."

Mair observed that there were other female mavericks worthy of recognition: "Cubah, Queen of Kingston, who men shipped out of the island but who found her way back and was executed; Teresa Constantine Phillips, 'Con', bright and literate . . . and Queen Nanny, who unlike Annie Palmer is firmly evidenced/located in the records. She was betrayed by black men who only got hand-me-down clothes as reward." Mair appealed for Nanny's status to be officially recognized in 1975, just as the UN International Decade for Women was about to be declared, and through her efforts, alongside fellow historian Kamau Brathwaite, Nanny was named a national heroine in Jamaica.

Mair's ideas, thoughts, philosophy and the content of her research were also shared through her numerous public lectures, speeches and seminar presentations, through her work at the United Nations, as a member of boards and committees, and in her professional capacity as a historian. Her speeches

and writings covered such topics as Jamaica's road to independence and the challenges of the immediate post-independence
period, when the focus on economic growth modelled on style
and strategy of Western industrial nations meant that the cri-
terion for development was a quantitative one. She lamented
the absence of qualitative criteria while people became poorer,
concluding that the Caribbean was left to pull itself up by its
own bootstraps without the masses possessing boots.[29]

Her concern about the inequitable economic order and the
impact of this inequity on women was frequently explored
in her work: "What we hope for is a glimpse into a possible
future world of greater equality of opportunities and economic
justice; a vision that can only be brought into focus by collective vision."[30] She maintained that the impact was greater on
women and explained why, locating women's condition within
the context of the slavery experience, when the enslaved population formed ninety-nine per cent of the labour force and
enjoyed zero per cent of the capital and zero per cent of the
prosperity on which the plantations were built. She argued
that blacks built the superstructure of the hemisphere; yet in
the new economic order the scenario after emancipation had
hardly changed.

She was critical of the structure of the world economy that
crippled the Global South and appealed for an understanding of
global interdependence and alternative development strategies
that would redress the gross North-South inequities. Despite
the mantra of globalization/interdependence, the rich were
exercising political and economic power over the poor, defeat-
ing the rhetoric of global partners. She championed regionalism

as a counter to these forces: "A strengthened and expanded regional base enables Jamaica and its CARICOM partners to participate with even more confidence and effectiveness in the larger and growing multilateral systems. We believe that multilateral diplomacy as an instrument of international cooperation, if thoroughly understood by small Third World nations, can influence international behaviour, can be a potent force in shaping regional, hemispheric and global concerns in a world of vast diversities and inequities: can, in fact, also facilitate bilateral relations."[31]

FOUR

The completion of her PhD thesis and her elevation in status as an academic in 1972 could be seen as a watershed in Mair's career. This achievement coincided with the ascendancy to government of Michael Manley's PNP and Manley's policy of recruiting a new cadre of experts from academia to bring fresh ideas to the new administration. It is unlikely that Mair would have escaped Manley's recruitment drive, given the close relationship they had shared from the time they were students in London. It is also reasonable to speculate that by 1973, after seventeen years at the helm of Mary Seacole Hall, Mair would have been ready for a career change and new challenges. While it is difficult to envisage the Mair we have so far seen in the daily cut and thrust of politics, her gentle, graceful exterior belied a steely reserve that made her an ideal candidate for the diplomatic career that would be her niche for the rest of her working life.

Mair's views on development, society, women and the region would grow stronger as she matured and gained experience, but these views had started with conversations on her grandfather's veranda, with meetings at the West Indian Students' Union in London, with intellectual discussions with her counterparts at the UWI and bright young minds at Mary Seacole Hall. She later became part of an informal political grouping that included Mavis Gilmour, Gloria Cumper, Leacroft Robinson, and Leo and Irena Cousins, which began meeting after the 1967 general election. Though it included former and then current members of the PNP and shared the party's philosophy and policy position on several social issues, it was not PNP-affiliated. The group did not engage in just "veranda talk" but produced broadcasts that were aired on radio. On occasion it invited guests to speak on issues of the day as well as broader political and social concerns.

Early in the 1970s, Michael Manley commissioned Mair to undertake a study of the conditions of women in Jamaica. Her research and the resulting report, complete with recommendations, formed the basis of a policy paper on women which became an essential part of the PNP platform in its campaign leading up to the general election of 1972. Dubbed a "Proposed Governmental Machinery for Improving the Condition of Women and Ensuring their Fullest Participation in Economic and Social Development", the document included a memorandum on the establishment of a women's bureau, which would be helmed by Mair's former UWI colleague Peggy Antrobus.

In conducting the fieldwork to prepare her report and recommendations, Mair visited several rural communities throughout the country. The experience of interacting with women in both rural and urban communities and at different socio-economic levels inevitably helped to increase her political awareness.

Her research and policy recommendations allowed the Manley administration to implement the kinds of initiatives that were needed. She also played an active role in the PNP Women's Movement alongside figures like Beverley Manley and Madame Rose Leon. In the process, she elevated and legitimized political activity as being a worthwhile endeavour for women of all classes and status.

Mair's first taste of the diplomatic life was when she represented Jamaica at the twenty-third session of the UN Commission for Social Development in 1973 and, immediately after, on the Economic and Social Committee, for which she served as vice-chair. It was while serving on this committee that she first came to notice as an advocate for the cause of Third World women.

In 1974, Mair served as the first executive director of the Agency for Public Information,[32] which she was instrumental in helping to set up, along with John Hearne, while on secondment from her substantive post as warden of Mary Seacole Hall. While in this position she received her first full-time diplomatic appointment, as Jamaica's deputy permanent representative to the United Nations, based in New York. In taking up this new assignment, Mair simply continued where she had left off, serving as chair of the Social, Humanitarian and Cultural Committee, also known as the Third Committee of the UN General Assembly. She served on that committee in 1973, 1975 and 1976. However, it was in her role as Jamaica's representative at the first ever Conference on the Status of Women in Mexico City in 1975, during the UN Decade for Women, that Mair made her mark by playing a leading role in drafting the seminal conference document: the 1975 Declaration of Mexico on the Equality of Women and Their Contribution to Development and Peace.

The Mexico City conference was a significant step in uniting women from across the world, especially from developing countries. Some of them, including Mair, were already active in the women's movements and were involved in the struggle to improve the conditions of women in their home countries.[33] Other outstanding Jamaican and Caribbean women present included Peggy Antrobus, Dame Nita Barrow (the first female governor general of Barbados) and Beverley Manley, president of the PNP Women's Movement and wife of Prime Minister Michael Manley.

Reflecting on the Declaration of Mexico and Mair's participation at the conference, Peggy Antrobus noted: "She understood, as few women did, the distinction between a technical plan of action and a declaration of political will. She also understood that one could not separate women from the broader context of their lives, and pushed for the inclusion in the Plan of Action of references to Apartheid and the plight of the Palestinians as well as the call for a New International Economic Order."[34]

Mair's activism led to her push for women to access development funding from the United Nations. She represented Latin America and the Caribbean on the Consultative Committee on the Voluntary Fund of the UN Decade for Women (later known as UNIFEM/UN Women), which afforded her the opportunity to draft the terms of reference and to establish alliances with small non-profit organizations. Reflecting years later on her experience at the Mexico City Conference as she prepared to lead the follow-up mid-decade conference in Copenhagen, Denmark, in 1980, Mair remarked:

> Five years ago in Mexico City the world conference of International Women's Year was held. It was a unique event, for while women from different parts of the world had been meeting on specific social issues for nearly a century, usually either under the aegis of non-governmental organisations or professional associations, on no previous occasion had women met as the representatives of their governments, nor to discuss the entire range of women's concerns. And that range, quite simply, encompassed the experience of all humanity.

She also highlighted the competing priorities that emerged within the context of the conference: "The Mexico conference was historical and it was the first time women from all over the world were representing their governments. . . . Unfortunately, it proved that the representatives from the 'i-countries' were discussing equality, those from 'dev countries', development, while the representatives from the East were talking about peace."[35]

Mair interrupted her service at the United Nations in 1978 to take up the post of ambassador to Cuba of the Government of Jamaica. This would have been a challenging yet interesting assignment for her, as her tour of duty came at the height of US hostility towards the Manley administration because of its association with Fidel Castro's communist regime in Cuba. Her frequent dispatches to the ministry kept the Jamaican government informed of developments in Cuba's Africa policy as it related to Angola, Zaire and Ethiopia, and the growing anti-imperialist sentiment in Africa.

Inevitably, she became involved in the Non-Aligned Movement, of which both Jamaica and Cuba were leading proponents, and in the course of her tour met students, teachers and other diplomats as well as a virtual who's who of the non-aligned/ socialist/communist movements from Asia, Latin America, Africa and Europe. In 1978 she served as rapporteur to the meeting of the Coordinating Bureau of the Non-Aligned Countries that was held in Havana.

Apart from her main responsibilities of handling the delicate regional, hemispheric and geopolitical issues that inevitably involved Cuba, the welfare of Jamaican students in Cuba was an important part of her portfolio. Her years as warden of Mary Seacole Hall prepared her well for this role. Many of the students experienced challenges in adjusting to life in Cuba, and their problems ranged from their living conditions and diet to concerns about living expenses. There were also thorny issues like the compulsory Marxist-Leninist component in the curricula and the insistence of some institutions on holding on to students' passports. Mair was sympathetic towards these students' concerns but at the same time suggested to the Ministry of Foreign Affairs that there was need for a more structured programme of orientation before the students embarked on their studies in Cuba.

In Cuba, Mair encountered a new gender dynamic, which she saw as a form of matriarchy. There was a high dependency on the reproductive and community roles of the woman, but this was infused with a type of machismo that she had not experienced before. Understanding and finding solutions to gender issues there became part of her mission and purpose in Cuba. Her work in this area was recognized in 1978, when she received the Organization of American States award for outstanding contribution to the development of women.

Mair was ambassador to Cuba for just one year, as in 1979 she was appointed a UN assistant secretary-general, with the primary responsibility of preparing and leading the Second World Conference of the UN Decade for Women in Copenhagen in 1980. This was a clear acknowledgement of her leadership and organizational skills displayed at the first conference in Mexico City and her elevated status as a member of the Jamaican diplomatic corps in the intervening years.

Beginning with this appointment and for the next five years, up to 1984, Mair reached the apogee of her career as an international civil servant in the UN system. In addition to being the leading figure at the Copenhagen conference, in this period she also acted as assistant secretary-general and special adviser to UN Children's Fund (UNICEF) on women's development, and later under-secretary-general, at that time the highest rank reached by a woman at the United Nations. Her leadership of the Copenhagen conference was a natural outcome of the recognition and respect she had earned among women advocates worldwide. More than any of her contemporaries, Mair was instrumental in placing women's issues on the agenda for discussion and policy initiatives for their empowerment at all major global fora. In the months leading up to the Copenhagen conference, she spoke in detail about the outcomes of the 1975 conference in Mexico City and the progress achieved since then, and her expectations for the forthcoming conference, concluding that "the goals of the Decade, viz., Equality, Development and Peace, still remain a far way from being fulfilled":

> It is true that we are within the sight of acquiring an international legal instrument, viz., a UN convention for the elimination of discrimination against women, which it is hoped can be finalized at the 34th session of the General Assembly, [and] thus can be the culmination of decades of struggle to equalise women's status before the law. But everyone is aware of the limitations of international legal instruments, which can remain paper instruments without national action to support them. We cannot, moreover, legislate for, or for that matter, against, attitudes, against that whole complex inheritance of human prejudices and instinctive responses to the image of woman – present in the minds and feelings of both men and women – and which perhaps fundamentally represent the strongest barriers to real equality. That is a legacy of centuries, which cannot be easily disposed of in a Decade. Development in its fullest sense eludes us.
>
> The Decade's goal for peace remains also an elusive goal. It underlines the irrationality of a world which finds it possible to budget so much more for destruction, and so little for development.[36]

In preparing for the conference in Copenhagen, Mair was responsible for assembling documents and chairing meetings. The conference aimed at uniting fifteen hundred women from across the world on issues ranging from peace in the Middle East and apartheid in South Africa to the Zionist movement in Palestine and the complex circumstances faced by women in both industrialized and developing countries. Her role was not only administrative; she also offered intellectual leadership to countries that were interested in implementing programmes of action in the UN Decade for Women. Her leadership was not without its challenges, given the political tensions that surrounded and characterized its proceedings. At the centre of these tensions was the contrasting priority and focus placed on the issues of apartheid and the status of Palestine as they affected women specifically by countries of the Third World compared to the position of the developed countries, the United States and Great Britain in particular.

Mair's diplomatic skills and the success of the Copenhagen conference did not go unnoticed, because shortly after, she was appointed secretary-general of the UN International Conference on the Question of Palestine, which carried with it the rank of under-secretary-general. The Jamaica *Daily Gleaner* (10 May 1982), in reporting on her appointment, observed that "her general elevation to the new rank of Under-Secretary General, is also the first time any woman has held that rank, and is in our view an honour to herself, to Jamaica, and perhaps most of all, an acceptance of the legitimate aspirations of the struggling women of the world".

The question of Palestine was a mandate responsibility of the League of Nations which was explicitly returned in 1947 to a successor organization, the United Nations. Mair saw the question of Palestine as

> one of the "sacred trusts of humanity", to quote the words of Count Carlo Sforza of Italy, and as such, it is a continuing moral responsibility of the highest order to all who cherish the goals and principles of the United Nations Charter and the universal Declaration of Human Rights. The Question of Palestine is central to the future of the United Nations; and this is not surprising. Palestine is ultimately something other than a place on earth

with special geopolitical importance. It is a corner of the globe endowed with meaning – the land of the prophets, the birthplace of Judaism and Christianity, and a region that is deeply cherished by Muslims throughout the world. Sacred geography makes it compelling for the community of nations to adopt more forcefully the cause of peace.

The conference took place from 29 August to 7 September 1983 and it was not without drama, involving security threats to delegates and to Mair herself, who had security guards sleeping at her doorsteps in the hotels as she travelled in the period leading up to the conference. Mair's long-time friend Irena Cousins recalls Mair's response to the situation and how she deftly made light of it, saying, "Can you imagine, mi dear, me with those handsome young men sleeping across the doorstep of my hotel room wherever I went in the world? And trotting behind me when I go to powder my nose?"[37]

In the weeks leading up to the start of the conference Mair faced harsh criticism from sections of the press corps that were unsympathetic to the Palestine Liberation Organization. Curtis T. Perkins reported that "the PLO haters were really there. And they, especially some women reporters, went after Ms Mair with a studied vengeance. But this capable woman in a scholarly and common-sense manner deflected their venom and calmly answered them." From her front-seat position, Mair observed that "it was the only conference in UN history that took place behind barbed wire with guns mounted for the entire duration of the event. It took place in Geneva because no individual member state was prepared to host a conference as potentially hostile as that one." She was philosophical but realistic in her assessment of the outcome, noting: "I survived. We didn't solve anything but I think we did a lot towards educating the world about the multi-dimensions of that little plot of land."[38]

Mair concluded her duties as under-secretary-general and secretary-general on the UN International Conference on the Question of Palestine on 1 May 1984, at the end of her two year contract. Several people questioned the decision of Secretary-General Javier Pérez de Cuellar not to renew it, especially as Mair had been named the first female under-secretary-general of the United Nations. It was a heavily publicized affair, which led several men and women alike to question the commitment of the United Nations to eliminating all forms of discrimination, including discrimination on the secretariat staff. Though the secretary-general promised to look into the matter, nothing came of the issue, as Mair would never again rise to that level within the United Nations.

This was not to be the end of her association with the United Nations, however. Between 1989 and 1995, she served in a number of advisory capacities, first as council member and later as chair and vice-chair of the UN University Council; vice-chair of the executive council of UNICEF; and a member of the secretary-general's advisory group for the Fourth World Conference on Women.

In assessing Mair's career as an international civil servant, the description of her as "the consummate diplomat" is most apt, particularly in light of the numerous obstacles she encountered as a woman throughout her career. Her response to the subtle challenges that women like herself face in the diplomatic world and the workplace in general was not just to overcome and prevail but to consciously push the boundaries and, in the process, open doors of opportunity for herself and other women. Her innate self-assurance and her imposing presence made her difficult to ignore. Mair faced criticism for her stance on the issue of women, but she was unflinching in her mission to change the status quo. She was not afraid to challenge the inherent male privilege and entitlement, but always did so in a respectful way based on moral certitude. At that first World Conference on Women in Mexico City in 1975, Mair was recognized by one commentator as a force to be reckoned with, characterizing her as being "loud and outspoken". A more accurate assessment of her performance was perhaps that provided by a journalist at the same conference, Rose Blenman, who described her as "not a loud-mouthed woman but one who possesses a quiet demeanour, a warm smile and [one who] speaks in exact and quiet tones" ("Sterling Mark Made by Mair", *Sunday Sun*, 7 July 1996, 2a).[39]

FIVE

air's distinguished later career as public servant and international diplomat was grounded in her earlier work in the field of Caribbean women's history and Caribbean feminist studies and in the major contribution she made to the establishment of gender studies as an academic discipline in the region. It can be argued that Mair's entire adult professional life was devoted to empowering women, dating back to her mentoring of young girls at St Joseph's Convent School in St Lucia. Her seventeen-year stewardship of several cohorts of young women as warden of Mary Seacole Hall, many of whom were to become feminists and leaders in their own right, speaks of an unbroken progression to the formal institutionalization of gender studies within academia, for which she helped lay the groundwork.

After her duties at the United Nations ended in 1984, Mair returned to Jamaica. By this time, the international women's movement had found local impetus through pioneering women such as Peggy Antrobus and Joycelin Massiah, who had begun the process of researching, teaching and institutionalizing women and development studies in the Caribbean. The UN

Decade for Women beginning in 1976 led to several regional initiatives, most importantly the establishment by governments of
the English-speaking Caribbean of the Women and Development
Unit as a regional agency within the Department of Extra-Mural Studies at the UWI to promote national programmes for
women's development. Other important initiatives included
a seminar in 1977 at the Jamaica Women's Bureau and Social
Welfare Training Centre that was attended by members of the
Caribbean Women's Association to discuss the integration of
women and development studies with teaching courses at the
UWI. The Caribbean Women's Association had earlier called
for the establishment of a Women's Desk at the CARICOM
Secretariat.

By 1980, when Mair as secretary-general chaired the UN
Mid-Decade Conference for Women in Copenhagen, and Caribbean women like Phyllis Coard had attended the non-govern-
mental organization forum and made their presence felt, the
Caribbean women's movement was in its ascendancy. The Wom-
en's Desk at CARICOM had become a reality and CARICOM
had introduced the CARICOM Triennial Award for outstanding
women, of which Mair was later an awardee.

The move towards the establishment of women and development studies at the UWI had as one of its components a research
project – the Women in the Caribbean Project – spearheaded
by Joycelin Massiah through the Institute of Social and Economic Research with the aim of using data collected through
that project to inform teaching. A funding source through
the Government of the Netherlands to develop courses was
identified by Rhoda Reddock, who was then studying at the

Institute of Social Studies at The Hague. Peggy Antrobus, who was head of the Women and Development Unit and the Jamaica Women's Desk, followed through with the negotiations. Thus the Women and Development Studies Project was born, a collaboration between the UWI, the Institute of Social Studies and the Internationaal Onderwijs Programma (International Education Programme), and it led to the later establishment of the Centre for Gender and Development Studies, now the Institute for Gender and Development Studies, which celebrated its twenty-sixth anniversary in 2019.

Mair was appointed first consultant regional coordinator for the project in 1985. Midway into the consultancy, at her request, the University Appointments Committee in May 1988 agreed to convert her short-term role from that of consultant to the post of regional coordinator for women and development studies at the professorial level. The appointment was made effective from January 1987 to September 1989.

A formal offer letter by Joycelin Massiah setting out the parameters of the consultancy and subsequent conversations with Peggy Antrobus detailed a plan of action that was aimed at the integration of women and development studies at the UWI and ultimately across the region. It was agreed that Mair would conduct a series of seminars and familiarize herself with developments on each of the UWI campuses through discussions with study groups and administrators as well as the Department of Extra-Mural Studies. The purpose of this short-term consultancy was to establish the basis for a programme of Women and Development Studies, with the aim of launching the programme by October 1985.[40]

Mair set out her own priorities for the consultancy as advocacy, interdisciplinary teaching, comparative analysis of international women's studies programmes and cross-campus consultations. She embarked on the task with administrative assistance from Louraine Emmanuel.

She envisioned a conceptual framework for women's studies that would transform the production of knowledge, establish its intellectual purpose and its relevance to academic scholarship, and develop applied research for relevant and effective action. She also identified the need for a curriculum that would build on existing initiatives, but one with a fresh focus. Among the support she believed the project needed was technical data, especially on gender and the economy, to support the scholarship to be produced, and external cooperation and collaboration with other institutions, including fundraising. These issues, ideas and plans featured in the discussions she held with the women and development studies groups and the administration on each campus.

All meetings deliberated first of all on the questions: Why women's studies? Where should the programme be located? Why institutionalize women's studies at the university level? What was the knowledge gap to be filled? Where and how should women's studies be incorporated within the university? As a result of her role in the UN Decade for Women, Mair ensured that the conclusions from that conference featured in the discussions, including the fundamental role of education. In those meetings, there were several contrasting views on institutionalizing women's studies. Some were against a separate programme which would "ghettoize" women's studies (as some felt had happened to black studies in the United States), preferring integration into existing programmes.

In her notes of the meetings, Mair raised her concerns regarding the validity of such questions as "Why women's studies?" and "Should it be institutionalized?". At that time, women's studies programmes and degrees were emerging all over the world, with the United States leading with a variety of offerings. In her view, women in the Caribbean had equally valid contributions to make to the feminist movement and the study of women in faculties and universities around the globe. She lamented the fact that Western scholarship rather than Third World scholarship had taken the lead role in developing influential theoretical concepts concerning sex roles. She also expressed concern that the majority of research and theory developed on women had been extrapolated largely from the evolution of Western capitalist economies and societies, with little consideration of the specific, distinct circumstances of women in Third World countries.

On the question of locating the programme in a university, in a speech in 1986, Mair outlined what she saw as the three main trends in institutionalizing women's studies:

> One, seeking autonomy as a separate degree-granting programme either at the undergraduate or post-graduate level, essentially an autonomous entity within the collegiate system: [two], working within traditional disciplines in the existing departments and there offering courses which reflect the data and theory generated by the new scholarship on women: third – a less precise, but a frequent approach – attempting to influence colleagues within academia to include material on women in their course

design and teaching. The latter two . . . reflect the phenomenon of "piggy backing". These are not mutually exclusive approaches and can in fact be mutually reinforcing.

On the question of how to position women's studies in the Caribbean, she expressed the view that maybe it should not be presented "so much *as political* (i.e. feminist), which may not be appropriate for University, but on grounds of enhancing knowledge", a view shared by several women in the academy.[41] But this view was obviously a strategy for getting support for a field that still faced resistance at the UWI in the 1980s, because by then Mair herself had no problem with feminism and many of the women who were involved in the establishment and development of the Centre (later, Institute) for Gender and Development Studies were proclaimed feminists.

The question of what she wanted to create also preoccupied her. She drew up possible topics for lectures, some of which came from her PhD thesis. She came up with a good definition of what women and development studies was about: "Women's Studies seek to adjust the parameters of knowledge and should be seen neither as threat nor nuisance." But the recipe, in her view, could not simply be "add women and stir . . . [unless] we are trying to cook up a storm". Other rhetorical questions she asked were: "Are we adding a feminine dimension to scholarship or are we transforming scholarship?" Her answer? "Both! The result – a healthy brew." She also outlined the three main goals of women's studies, namely, to eliminate errors of fact about women and correct the record; add knowledge about women; and to look where we have not looked before. "More ambitious, more challenging as a consequence of eliminating inaccuracies, is increasing our knowledge base [because] we have to honestly and courageously rethink . . . analyse, and construct new theories."

At the end of her first round of consultations on the three campuses, Mair's own assessment was that there was broad agreement and an emerging consensus about the need for and thrust of the programme. The decisive breakthrough came with her presentation to the university's Planning and Estimates Committee at Mona in March 1985, at which she tabled reports on her visit and discussions at St Augustine and Cave Hill campuses, the status of negotiations with the Institute of Social Studies and fundraising, among other matters. She refused to accept a negative response from Vice Chancellor A.Z. Preston, but pressed on until she convinced him to support the integration of a women and development studies programme into the UWI.

Both Joycelin Massiah and Elsa Leo-Rhynie were present at the meeting and they attest to the effectiveness of Mair's presence and presentation. Massiah was impressed by her advocacy role, which she assumed in respect of the senior colleagues in the administration, and her infusion of enthusiasm and hope for the three campus groups. Leo-Rhynie declared that "the hour we spent in Dr Preston's office was one of the most valuable learning experiences I've had in diplomacy and negotiation". Mair "brought her case, she acknowledged his feelings, she understood his reasoning; but at the same time, she had to put forward her position. She felt that in the global sphere and the global environment, women's studies were very important; and for the UWI to be left behind would be so terrible. After all, we wouldn't be asking the University for money – we were bringing our own money. It was amazing."[42]

Mair was well aware of the task she had undertaken as well as the collective work that had gone on before and was to come. In a 1985 speech, she explained that women's studies in the Caribbean

> constitutes one of the most challenging, dynamic, and potentially rich areas of research and scholarship in the region. It could not be otherwise for it is a collective enterprise with a group of Caribbean women and men, nearly all of them bright, creative and quite wonderful. Before they are all through, what a difference they will make to what we teach and how we teach on the campuses of Mona, Cave Hill and St Augustine, and what we carry into society.[43]

She also mulled over the issue of a professional programme that would integrate law, government/politics, economics, history, sociology, English and education; but she was clear that "the project is *not* area studies (c.f. Black Studies) which would equal marginalization".

Mair rejected any notion that the region pioneered the field, but was insistent that the inherited narratives had to be indigenized as the Caribbean sought to embark on its own journey:

> We [in the Caribbean] belong to the International Women's Movement. Our part in this movement has seen an outpouring of scholarship mostly from the Northern Academy. Is the scholarship relevant to the Caribbean? This of course is a familiar dilemma. We can do an inventory; accept and reject. As independent people we can view what emanates from the metropole with much objectivity. We have already seen shifts in the area of

economics – challenge to classic notions of labour etc. We need
to expand knowledge on how Third World women really live.[44]

Funding constraints and the short period (four years) that
she spent in the post as regional coordinator meant that not all
that Mair had envisioned had come to fruition. Nevertheless,
she was pleased with her contributions. Four years after her
resignation, she remarked in a speech, "the programme is now
poised to move from the periphery of the academy to a Centre
of Gender and Development Studies".[45]

Mair's role in the establishment of the Centre for Gender
and Development Studies, which was to become the Institute
for Gender and Development Studies in 1993, has always been
hailed; and those who joined the institute after the work of the
pioneers have tried to carry on the legacy. The time she spent
developing the programme had resulted in the completion of
the first phase of the project. The stage was set for the project to
operate autonomously of the Institute of Social Studies, standing
on its own as an independent centre of research and learning
within the university.[46] Mair's contribution to the establishment
of women and development studies at the UWI has, since 1998,
been recognized by way of a lecture series named in her honour.

SIX

In 1989 came what might be described as Mair's third career: an appointment to Jamaica's upper house of Parliament, the Senate, and as minister of state in the Ministry of Foreign Affairs and Foreign Trade. Her contributions in senate debates covered a wide range of issues, from women and development to the need to combat environmental degradation, beach erosion and deforestation. She addressed Jamaica's sensitivity as a small island developing state to the increasing effects of climate change and the need for the pursuance of external relations with other countries, specifically with the wider Caribbean. She believed that the Caribbean region stood taller and stronger in the international arena and suggested that relationships with CARICOM member states should be the cornerstone of foreign policy in the 1990s. In a 1991 speech on climate change and the need for a regional approach, she said:

> In my little island, which is only one of the thirteen specks in the Caribbean Sea, we are learning more and more that no island is an island, only parts of the vast continent of the space planet. We're learning the hard way that whatever resources we may

each have, physical or human or whatever, can only be of value if it becomes part of a coordinated collective effort to make our region a zone of peace.[47]

Mair also addressed the issue of the need for small states and countries in the developing world to form regional and international lobby groups, and the necessity to develop relations in analysis of national priorities in order to stay afloat in the international economic system. In her State of the Nation presentation in 1989 she declared, "For as the world turns, [as] we see it now turning, it is conceivable that the future may no longer be the danger of nuclear war, but rather the collective consequence of Third World underdevelopment, the collective struggling under the burden of massive indebtedness."[48]

Mair's service as a lawmaker and government minister highlights her rounded contribution in the final years of the decade of the 1980s and into the 1990s. Furthermore, it ensured a continued association with the United Nations, as the portfolio she carried automatically made her a member of Jamaica's delegation to the General Assembly of the United Nations. Her stint as a legislator was a comparatively brief one but, in many ways, served as a preparation for her final diplomatic assignment to the United Nations in 1992, when she was appointed Jamaica's permanent representative to the world body. She tendered her resignation both as senator and minister of state on 31 January 1992 and moved to New York shortly after.

The respect and admiration she had gained from fellow senators were reflected in a special sitting of that chamber, in which tributes came from both sides of the floor. Mair's former colleague legislators had expressed confidence that she would continue to serve Jamaica well in her new role as the country's permanent representative to the United Nations and make her mark in that position.

As Jamaica's permanent representative to the United Nations for those few years, Mair continued her advocacy for women's rights, environmental issues, and peace and international security. During a conference held in The Hague in 1993, she expressed strong views on the topic of population control, the environment and women:

> Women had been brought in as it were through the back door into a global environment debate and presented as largely responsible for environmental degradation. This is the population issue, the thesis of the dangerous pressure of too many people, particularly of the third world, on the earth's fragile resources. Women, however, refuse to be cast as the villains of the piece and challenge the thesis that excessive third world birth rates account for environmental decay. On the contrary, women of the third world have a greater role in subsistence agriculture than any other group in their society.[49]

Mair was outspoken in her views on the United Nations and its charter, which reaffirms "faith in the equal rights of women and men", including the principle of observing gender equity in the establishment of its principal subsidiary organs. Contrary to this, she said in 1992, this principle was "more honoured in the breach itself than in the observance". On the topic of her own elevation to high rank, she said,

> It was 37 years after the signing of the charter before the first female Under-Secretary-General was appointed in the Secretariat. I have had the honour and privilege to be that female. At

the time there was, understand[ably,] the expectation that this would be the beginning of new enlightened policies acknowledging women's equal capabilities with men at all levels. Ten years later not only has there been no progress but rather regression as there is not even one woman holding a post at that level in the Secretariat. One could be forgiven for declaring that for women in the Secretariat, this has been a lost decade.[50]

Mair's appointment as permanent representative turned out to be her last. In less than three years that brilliant career would come to an end with her recall from the Permanent Mission of Jamaica to the United Nations because of debilitating ill-health. She formally retired from public life in 1995, interrupting her plans to dedicate her retirement years to the revision and publication of her PhD thesis.

SEVEN

The term "rebel woman" attached to Nanny of the Maroons and other ancestral women has also been unambiguously attached to Mair, even as she introduced us to these historical rebel women. Of course, not all rebel women take part in armed struggle, march, brandish placards and disrupt events, even though those are legitimate strategies of protest. Mair was to note that "in some cases, the activism may be intellectual and conceptual . . . an activism designed to free *self* from the circumscription, and even guilt, of the domestic . . . and . . . professional place, from the judgement of an established male hierarchy, even her peers, among whom she remains the unequal among equals. She is demanding a new structure to replace the old hierarchical ones."[51] Mair's rebellion was manifested differently from that of the historical rebel women but it was no less effective a driver for change. She used the lessons of history in the fight against gender injustice in postcolonial societies.

Among Mair's influences must be counted the Jamaican, Barbadian and Guyanese heritage of her parents, which no doubt helped to inform her firm belief in Caribbean integration, buttressed in later years through interaction with Caribbean people in her international assignments. Her work as a diplomat also exposed her to different cultures, expanded her world view and, along with her early exposure to classism, racism and skin-colourism in colonial Jamaica, made her abhor racism and intolerance. In addition, her father and stepfather were pan-Africanists, and her father a Garveyite and member of the New Negro Renaissance of the 1920s. She would have read her father's critically acclaimed *Tropic Death*, which, among other issues, addressed skin colour and class.

History education further shaped Mair's consciousness and ideology, starting with the early influence of her high school history teacher at Wolmer's, and further encouraged by her stepfather. Her views on colonialism, development and women's rights were formed through interaction with great thinkers and activists whom she met in London. At the UWI, she met writers in the Black Power movement who were calling for pan-Africanism, black empowerment and social equality, and engaged in deep philosophical conversations with brilliant minds on the Mona campus, including Walter Rodney. She also benefited from the political education she received in the PNP Women's Movement.

The knowledge she gained from the process of writing her PhD thesis and her keen insight into the ways in which contemporary societies were affected by the past informed Mair's views and actions. She demonstrated the usefulness and revolutionizing potential of the methodology of "women's history". The academic culture at the time seemed assured that there was no urgency to research issues surrounding the experiences of women in any way other than the most general. The manner in which women's history had an impact on popular perceptions and institutional determinations with respect to women's ascribed second-class citizenship was understood but not discerned as a crisis of postcolonial nationalism. Few scholars were willing to argue that this posture was a formidable part of the eruptive male intellectual leadership; and fewer still offered generalizations about the role of historiography within the reproduction of the patriarchal machinery of domination and exploitation. The few were female, and Mair was one of them. She historicized all topics she covered in her numerous lectures, speeches and opinion pieces and passed on the importance of history education to students and all those seeking a more liberating narrative of self.

The question has been asked if it was feminism that brought Mair to the topic of her thesis. That does not appear to be so, for she did not at first define herself as a feminist. In describing her motivation for choosing to do her thesis on women, she admitted that when she embarked on researching and writing women back into history: "I had no feminist motivation, or at least none that I recognized. I was motivated mainly by intellectual inquisitiveness, the usual ambition of the doctoral candidate to investigate virgin territory, which it was at that time." However, what Mair found in the pages of history as she tried to "decode the mysteries of the black female condition" would not only outrage her and make her wonder at what previous historians had ignored, but forced her to become a feminist, as her life after 1974 demonstrated.[52]

Her reflective piece "Recollections of a Journey into a Rebel Past" is the clearest statement of the evolution of her thinking about a range of issues that shaped her consciousness: "Wonderful things happened on the journey into that rebel past, of which Nanny became the permanent, powerful icon. I can here only briefly indicate the personal process of self growth it meant. No one could spend so many years in the company of such women and remain the same. The expansion of one's emotional and intellectual resources, the deepened pride in one's inheritance and in one's womanhood were inevitable."[53]

She was impressed by the evidence in the archival records of the rebel woman who did not sit back and endure her condition uncomplainingly and she became one of them. She saw her work with Kamau Brathwaite to provide the Jamaican government with the historical data that resulted in Nanny of the Maroons being included in the pantheon of national heroes of Jamaica in 1975 almost as the triumph of her academic life: "More relevant was the great occasion when a personal conviction about Nanny's profound significance to the Jamaican psyche became a public reality."

She found parallels with Nanny's life and the lived experiences of other rebel women, such as Winnie Mandela, who with Nelson Mandela visited Jamaica in 1991. At a luncheon in Winnie's honour, Mair said,

> Your rebel spirit summons up for us the spirit of our African ancestral national heroine, Nanny. Nearly three centuries ago Nanny ruled our Portland mountains, [during] the terror of a white regime, which would, if it could, put chains on the minds and bodies of every man and woman of this island who was of

African descent. . . . Today we celebrate your defiance of the
twentieth century version of such a regime.[54]

Mair never tried to convert anyone to feminism, but she
was impatient with people who declared they did not associate
themselves with women's liberation without justifiable reasons
and a clear understanding of what feminism was. She made
no secret of her ideas, opinions and the causes she supported:

> The fact that I happen to be absolutely comfortable being called a
> feminist or a supporter of Women's Liberation (assuming I have to
> be called something), does not mean I am presumptuous enough
> to suggest or recommend that other women must be equally
> comfortable with those labels. What I do, however, suggest, is
> that a woman or a group that consciously rejects association
> with anything named Women's Liberation owes it to herself as a
> thinking being, owes it to her organization, to understand clearly
> the process of rejection.[55]

She was not afraid to call out men for gender bias. She related
the case of a woman friend of hers who was writing for a local
media organization. Her friend submitted, among other ideas,
a story that revolved around feminism. But the male head of
the organization responded, "I would be grateful if you would
refrain from introducing the subject of women's liberation into
this firm. We do not wish to import any sick, North American
phenomenon into our island, especially as Jamaican women
have always held such a special elevated position." Mair's wry
reply to this was

> Women, not you Mr Media, should define what women are. They
> should say if they hold the position you say they hold. . . . A new
> deal for women in Jamaica must start here – self-definition. We

trot out the matriarch and female head of household in Jamaica and equate that with power. Look at the jobs they do to maintain their households? They are not high paying but mainly service/low pay. Whether at University or [in] firms high roles go to the men.[56]

These issues of gender justice and gender equality infused Mair's speeches and actions inside and outside of Jamaica and the Caribbean. She argued that, for the most part, on paper and in constitutions, and certainly since 1944 in the case of Jamaica, gender equality existed, but that the reality of what women experienced was far from what was promised. In her Human Rights Day lecture in 1974, she made this controversial statement: "If we look at women's roles historically we see that they played a far more important role than their present roles would suggest. So decolonization has in some ways turned back their pre-independence importance. Those who would seek to confine women to a certain sphere, despite their historic contributions should let history lead them."[57]

Mair was particularly concerned about the economic status of women who had played such a vital role in the economics of slavery and emancipation but in the post-slavery period experienced economic, social and political marginalization. It was clear to her that a new deal for women was needed: "Women's economic condition is critically determined by the overall structure of society, in particular, their economic condition is determined by the level of national development which in our increasingly inter-dependent world is also a reflection of global economic relationships."[58]

Not surprisingly, she expressed the view that women should not be marginalized in the process of development. In a memorandum sent to then prime minister Michael Manley ("Women and Social Change", 18 July 1972), Mair painted a clear picture of what her ideology was with regard to women's economic welfare. She did not believe that it was possible (or wise) to construct a nation or seek development status without the input of women, especially as more and more, women were given and took opportunities to explore the "upper levels of education", not only completing secondary school, but also pursuing tertiary education.

Throughout her career, Mair used her platform as a means of lobbying for women's rights and for the prioritization of women's affairs to be included in the development agenda. Quoting the executive director of UNICEF at a meeting of the Social Committee of the UN Economic and Social Council in 1981, she reminded her audience that "a woman's right to share whatever fruits the process of economic development has to offer is absolutely fundamental to all her roles. It is her poverty above all which is making her an 'inadequate mother', not her social behaviour, her illiteracy, her limited horizons or her exhausting workload, all of which are merely factors of that poverty."[59]

Women' reproductive rights formed part of her feminist activism. But she blamed "foreign propaganda and religious groups for daring to inform women about what was good for us". While she acknowledged the role that dominant faiths play in advancing or expanding women's status, she still considered religious fundamentalism a hindrance to the progress of women in seeking equality and in the full enjoyment of their basic human rights, including reproductive rights.

She saw too the possibilities for creative women to be agents of change: "The creative woman of the Third World must discover and define self within the context of defining and discovering or re-discovering the cultural and political formations with which she functions. Changing societies is not for her a peripheral but a central concern. It is even more urgent for black women whose ancestors enslavers tried to erase from memory, but whose stories survived and aided creative women attempting to change culture and society." The women who embodied this force included Louise Bennett, who was attempting to influence nation language; Margaret Walker, who put down roots and celebrated them long before Alex Haley; and Brazilian slum dweller Carolina Maria de Jesus, "who on scavenged scraps of paper could affirm black hair is good hair": "For the Third World Woman, then, creativity is a tool of liberation for herself and her society; the bridge of beyond which she invested with the spirit of survival."[60]

Mair was always insistent that her deep concern for women and for the advancement of women's and girls' rights should never be confused with extremism or anti-male sentiments:

> If I could say something briefly about the role of men vis a vis the creative woman, my own view is very simple. I know from experience of the profound misogyny (dislike of, contempt for, or ingrained prejudice against women) of many men and in particular of many competitive, creative men. However, I would also like to say that some of the most supportive and most inspiring creative persons of my acquaintance are also men, whose creative range and generosity are a source of both stimulation and support. And I feel that if as women we need to have man the

enemy as a foil for our creativity, we may well be creating another trap for ourselves.[61]

Among the men for whom Mair expressed admiration were her stepfather, and Norman and Michael Manley. She was hard-hit by Michael's death, reflecting on their time in London when "we also shared our hopes for and our commitment to that new independent Jamaica being pioneered by Norman Manley". She stressed that "the life and work of father and son (Norman and Michael Manley) were inspired by passionate commitment to justice and to the equality of all human beings, regardless of class, nationality, race or sex. They both challenged imperial-ism, colonialism, racism, sexism. Yes, sexism, that virtually universal phenomenon [which] labelled women second sex, and regions around the world established her status as such."[62]

During the Decade for Action to Combat Racism, she made a statement that remains relevant today: "the elimination of racism is the most intractable problem facing the international family today".[63] She often spoke about the colonial legacies that allowed racism to fester. The constructs of Eurocentricity used to poison and colonize Africa and Africans never penetrated Mair's mind, as, through her own inner consciousness and through her continued research on pre-colonial African society, she discovered and spread the truth. She wrote: "If, indeed, as has been argued, their ancient culture was 'the shield which frustrated the efforts of Europeans to dehumanise Africans through servitude' it can also be argued that it was the Afri-can woman's perception of herself within that culture, which accompanied her across the Middle Passage, and which helped to preserve her from total defeminization in the New World."[64]

Mair's uncompromising opposition to colonialism and its racist legacies made her an anti-apartheid activist. She used every opportunity to include in her presentations the issue of the apartheid regime in South Africa and the independence movement in Namibia, which, at the time, was under threat from South African imperialists.

She was both a nationalist and a committed regionalist. She demonstrated a devout sense of loyalty to Jamaica's neighbours and allies, especially in cases of national crises, like those that took place in Haiti and across Latin America in the 1980s and 1990s. In a speech in 1988, she said: "We have no choice but to pool our resources and convert our theses and declarations on the benefits of regional integration into a functioning strategy, to give bite and teeth to the provision of the Treaty of Cha-guaramas; to make CARICOM a truly effective instrument of integration." She viewed CARICOM as the "springboard for multilateral effectiveness", and expressed frequently a desire for Jamaica to prioritize relationships with organizations such as CARICOM, the G-77 and the Commonwealth. She was com-mitted to the non-aligned movement and was never afraid to speak out in support of Cuba and Palestine and against US actions towards them.[65]

Mair also turned her critical lens on development, more specifically international development and the auspices under which it should be considered and achieved. She supported a search for new development models that were appropriate to postcolonial societies in the Global South, that is, models that did not overlook human and political development in the interest of trade barriers and international debt. She understood that political development was necessary for human development so that people could be afforded the chance to choose those who handled resources. But that meant putting in place responsible governments to steer the ship; in this regard she constantly argued for greater representation of women in politics.

She was critical of international financial institutions, which, as partners to the United Nations, had the responsibility to address issues such as poverty and unemployment. She argued strongly that these institutions should pay attention to the social content of their fiscal policies of structural adjustment. She believed that even security should be redefined to include the human element rather than just the militaristic. She was clear that focus should be placed on disarmament and spending on social amenities in order to achieve human security. In a 1991 speech she asked whether the United Nations could now "shift gears and revitalise itself to meet the demands of a world no longer dominated by East-West bipolarity, but faced with potentially threatening evidence of intensified North-South disparities".[66]

In this same speech, she also made an unusual link between peace and security and the environment in Third World countries:

> Analyses of today's threats take more and more into account those non-military, socio-economic issues such as resource needs of water, land, oil, movements of people, demands for human rights, which constitute a "silent war" and underline the fact that security in the modern world can neither be completely defined in military terms nor can it be insured through military means. . . . With a fundamental shift in our definition of security, which

now includes the destabilising consequences of environmental degradation, famine, drought, displacement of people, and we should add the new interstate disease, AIDS, the UN must accordingly adjust its priorities and its modus operandi.[67]

Mair used every opportunity to express the viewpoint that since the classical age of colonization, the condition in the south had not changed much. On the contrary, the structure of the world economy had crippled the Global South and she constantly appealed for an understanding of global interdependence and alternative development strategies and the postcolonial condition.

EIGHT

Mair died on 28 January 2009, about six months shy of her eighty-fifth birthday, leaving her family, a host of friends, former colleagues and admirers to mourn her passing. When a complete history of the formal integration of women as important actors in national, regional and international development is written, Mair will stand out as one of the champions in a movement that is ongoing and constantly in need of new champions. Whether it was as the intellectual force behind the mainstreaming of women's affairs as an essential component of development in her native Jamaica or as the "mother" of gender and development studies within the academy in the Caribbean or as the quiet, dignified but decisive de facto leader in the fight for women's rights on the international stage for more than a decade, Mair blazed a trail of achievement for generations of women to follow.

It is no exaggeration to say that among the acknowledged pioneers in the process of women's empowerment in the Caribbean, she, above all others, dedicated her entire adult life to this cause until she was prematurely cut down by a debilitating illness. Such is the fate of brilliant minds felled by the dreaded Alzheimer's disease. It was the closing chapter of the remarkable career of an outstanding architect of Caribbean culture. One who, as the Institute for Gender and Development Studies reminded us on her passing, "contributed to the nation's recognition of the need for us to develop a respect for our cultural heritage and diversity, including the particular culture of women".[68]

In assessing Mair's lifelong contribution to Caribbean development, it is important to emphasize her advocacy for and leadership of women as equal actors. She was "a leader of women for women in a man's world".[69] Many were inspired by her advocacy and willingness to act as a mentor to the young. Equal importance must also be placed on her intellectual prowess and her multifaceted life's work, from introducing elements of Caribbean history into the school curriculum of St Joseph's Convent, her first teaching job in St Lucia in the 1950s, to heading Jamaica's mission to the United Nations in the 1990s. Within that career it is possible to identify her outstanding contributions in the areas of social inclusion, equality and governance; international diplomacy; feminist epistemology; Caribbean colonial and postcolonial history; visual and performing arts; and the mentoring of young women.

As a woman with deep-rooted Caribbean attachments – familial, professional and social – Mair was unequivocally clear about her belief in the need for the countries in the region to cooperate and integrate, especially within the postcolonial context. Her marriages, her role in establishing a cross-Caribbean institute, and her lifelong friendships are a testament to this belief. It is no wonder that Dame Nita Barrow, the first female governor general of Barbados, once encouraged Mair to "continue to be your indomitable self".

Her role as an international public servant was universally lauded. In its tribute at the time of her death, the *Gleaner* (2 February 2009) described Mair as "a scholar of great intellectual stature, a diplomat and international public servant who worked with diligence to advance and improve the status of women, not only in Jamaica and the Caribbean, but throughout the world".

Throughout her career she consistently supported the maxim, "nothing about us without us", "us" in this context meaning women, women in the developing world and developing countries. Her commitment to these causes was clear throughout her career.

At the celebration of her life on 6 February 2009 at the chapel on the Mona campus of the UWI, she was eulogized as "hard-working, charismatic and a champion for women", sentiments reiterated by Ban Ki Moon, then secretary-general of the United Nations, and others in the tributes at her funeral. In the words of Peggy Antrobus in her tribute, "She inspired a multigenerational network of women, and many men as well, bringing us into the historic struggle for gender justice, in Lucille's own words, to create 'a consciousness of women as significant beings' as a first step toward the transformation of relationships of power between men and women leading to a more caring, humane and just world."

In a tribute published in the *Stabroek News* (9 February 2009), Alissa Trotz, director of Caribbean studies at the University of Toronto, highlighted Mair's feminist commitment and work in the area of gender, also reiterating this author's description of Mair's "unstinting dedication to women's equality" because she "put the difficult question of difference on the table as a feminist issue from the start". Honor Ford-Smith, performer, teacher and founding artistic director of the Jamaican women's group Sistren, said in her tribute that "Mair's forwardness and example inspired many Caribbean women to name themselves in public space as feminists and to draw on regional histories for a foundation of committed feminist practice".

Mair's roles as a revisionist historian, academic and women's rights advocate went hand in hand, as she used her thesis and her writings not only as a way of rewriting women into the annals of history, but re-establishing the roles that women played in the resistance movements, and reinforcing the urgency of researching issues surrounding the experiences of women. Nothing escaped her careful eye; no action was too small or too insignificant for her to discuss, especially when formulating ideas about women's agency.

Her work did not go unrewarded. Throughout her illustrious career, Mair was recognized with numerous awards and citations, among them the CARICOM Triennial Award for Women (1996), a degree of doctor of laws, honoris causa, UWI (1993), and an honorary doctorate of humane letters from the University of Florida (1988). The Organization of American States named her a "Woman of Distinction" in 1978; she received the Centennial Silver Medal of the Institute of Jamaica for her contribution to art in 1979; and she received an honorary fellowship from the Institute of Social Studies, The Hague, in 1988. She was twice bestowed with Jamaican national honours:

the Order of Distinction (Commander Class) in 1980 and the Order of Jamaica in 1996.

Many of these framed awards, plaques and citations can be found in her home in Norbrook, St Andrew, Jamaica, as her children continue to memorialize her and preserve her legacy through a vast collection of works of art as well as writings and hundreds of books. Among the collection are several letters, cards and newspaper clippings, several of which were sent as congratulatory messages from her friends and colleagues – national, regional and international – who, while not surprised by them, never took her awards and honours for granted. Her receipt of the national honour of Order of Jamaica brought a touching congratulatory note from her long-time friend and colleague Michael Manley: "You have made a splendid contribution – to Jamaica, to the Caribbean and to the world through the U.N. In all this you have been, like our great friend Nita [Barrow], a pioneer in the movement that is increasingly demolishing the barriers that kept women from their true place in the running of the world."

At the ceremony in Barbados in 1996 to receive the CARICOM Triennial Award, Mair declared that she accepted the award not just for herself but also for the men and women who made it possible. She singled out Sir Philip Sherlock, Elsa Goveia, Sir Arthur Lewis, Michael Manley and Dame Nita Barrow, remarking that "there are stages in your life when you have to pay tribute to those who, in offering guidance, inspiration and encouragement made things possible for you".[70]

It is critical to remember the importance of this rebel woman who over the course of her life worked her heart out for the cause of Caribbean freedom; who popularized the power of history education for all those seeking a more liberating narrative of self; who participated in the work needed for the institution-alization of gender studies at the UWI; who was never afraid to speak truth to power and stand her ground, especially as a senator and at the United Nations; who lobbied for gender justice for all women, social justice for those who occupy the spaces in the Global South and representation at the diplomatic level for a new development model. She helped us all to understand that a culture which reinforces feelings of inferiority continues to negatively affect Caribbean women, while acknowledging that women have nevertheless made significant strides towards equality.

In a cruel twist of fate, Mair forgot her own importance towards the end of her life. On visiting her in the days before her condition worsened, Peggy Antrobus remarked: "Whatever the distance her illness created we could still see beyond the frail body to the person, feel her warmth, experience her smile and sometimes laugh about our times together." As Antrobus tells it, when she spoke to her about the "good ole days" and of all the work they had done together, Mair looked at her and said, "Peggy, you mean I did all that?"[71]

NOTES

1. Lucille Mair, undated journal (private collection). Unless otherwise indicated, all quotes from Mair are from her journals and notes in her personal papers.

2. Wade and Parascandola, introduction to *Eric Walrond*.

3. Parascandola and Davis, "A West Indian", 189; Frederick, "Genre, Gender", 109.

4. In New York, Walrond was an early champion of Black Nationalism and was a member of the Marcus Garvey Movement, serving as associate editor of *Negro World*, the journal of the Universal Negro Improvement Association. Along with others such as Langston Hughes and the Jamaican novelist Claude McKay, Walrond became a central figure in the Harlem Renaissance, that group of black writers and artists who flourished in New York in the early twentieth century.

5. Lucille Mathurin Mair, interview by Edward Baugh, New York, September 1993.

6. Henry Fowler is best remembered as the founder and headmaster of the Priory School in Kingston, of which Mair became a board member.

7. Clark Cousins, interview with Stephanie Sewell, Kingston, Jamaica, May 2018.

8. Mair, interview by Baugh.

9. Sonia Mills, interview by Stephanie Sewell, Kingston, Jamaica, May 2018.

10. Baugh, *Chancellor*.

11. Peter Josie, "Jamaicans Who Provided Sterling Service to Saint Lucia (Part One)", *St Lucia Star*, 18 March 2017.

12. Ibid.

13. Velma Pollard, interview by Stephanie Sewell, Kingston, Jamaica, December 2017. All quotes from Pollard are taken from this interview.

14. Marjorie Whylie, interview by Stephanie Sewell, Kingston, Jamaica, June 2018.

15. Patricia Durrant, telephone interview by Stephanie Sewell, January 2018.

16. Mair, "The Student and the University's Civilising Role". Subsequent references appear parenthetically in the text.

17. Lucille Mathurin Mair, "Creative Women in Changing Societies" (speech delivered at the seminar Creative Women in Changing Societies, Oslo, Norway, 1980).

18. Nettleford, *From the Heart*, 194.

19. Mair, "Jamaican Women".

20. Beckles and Shepherd, introduction to Mair, *Historical Study*, xiv.

21. Quoted in Lewis, *Walter Rodney*, 24.

22. A reference to the title of Kamau Brathwaite's trilogy of linked poems exploring the history of black people in the Caribbean and the African diaspora.

23. Mair had taken tentative steps towards publication not long after she finished – including creating a plan for reorganizing the structure and asking colleagues such as Barry Higman for advice – and there had been a contract with a US publisher in the 1980s, but her responsibilities once she left academia meant she had little time to complete the work needed. Mair later asked this writer

and Hilary McD. Beckles to edit and revise the manuscript, which was published in 2006 by the University of the West Indies Press.

24. Bolles, review, 126.

25. Originally published by the Institute of Jamaica in 1975, it was reprinted by the University of the West Indies Press in 2007. Recent thinking about the name "Nanny" is that the more respectful Twi word for venerable ancestor, elder or leader in a high office, "Nana", should be used for this Maroon warrior instead of a word that suggests someone engaged in childcare.

26. Mair, *Rebel Woman*, v.

27. Mair, "Commentary on the Ethics", 57.

28. Annie Palmer's Rose Hall mansion is a popular tourist attraction in Jamaica.

29. Lucille Mathurin Mair, speech delivered at the United Nations, New York, 6 May 1976.

30. Lucille Mathurin Mair, speech delivered at the Roundtable on Strategy for the 1980s, 13 June 1980.

31. Lucille Mathurin Mair, contribution to the State of the Nation debate, 21 October 1989.

32. The Agency for Public Information replaced and expanded the Jamaica Information Service, which has since reverted to that name.

33. For more details, see Stienstra, *Women's Movements*.

34. Peggy Antrobus, tribute to Lucille Mathurin Mair (University of the West Indies Chapel, Mona, Jamaica, 6 February 2009).

35. Lucille Mathurin Mair, speech delivered at the seminar "Progress of Equality with Particular Relevance to Programme for World Conference", Stockholm, Sweden, 12 April 1980.

36. Lucille Mathurin Mair, speech delivered at the Conference of Non-Aligned and Developing Countries on the Role of Women in Development, Baghdad, May 1979.

37. Irena Cousins, interview by Stephanie Sewell, Kingston, Jamaica, May 2018.

38. Curtis T. Perkins, "A Great Woman Secretary General Takes on a Thankless Task", *Torch Bearer* 4, no. 32 (10 September 1983): 1.

39. Blenman argues that Mair left a lasting impression on the United Nations and specifically Pérez de Cuellar from as early as the 1975 Mexico City conference, later contributing to the decision to ask her to lead the Copenhagen (1980) and Palestine (1983) conferences.

40. Peggy Antrobus, letter to Joycelin Massiah, September 1984

41. Lucille Mathurin Mair, "Perspectives on Women's Studies" (speech delivered at the fourth annual Symposium of the Women's Studies Group, University of the West Indies, Mona, Jamaica, December 1986).

42. Elsa Leo-Rhynie, telephone interview by Stephanie Sewell, Kingston, Jamaica, January 2018.

43. Lucille Mathurin Mair, "Women's Studies and the Academy" (speech, March 1985).

44. Lucille Mathurin Mair, "Women's Studies and the Academy" (speech, March 1985).

45. Lucille Mathurin Mair, speech delivered at the fortieth anniversary conference of the Institute of Social Studies, The Hague, January 1993.

46. Massiah, Leo-Rhynie and Bailey, *UWI Gender Journey*, 93.

47. Lucille Mathurin Mair, speech delivered at Grambling State University, Grambling, Louisiana, 8 April 1991.

48. Lucille Mathurin Mair, contribution to the State of the Nation debate, Kingston, Jamaica, 27 October 1989.

49. Lucille Mathurin Mair, speech delivered at the fortieth-anniversary conference of the Institute of Social Studies, The Hague, Netherlands, January 1993.

50. Lucille Mathurin Mair, statement delivered at the substantive session of the UN Economic and Social Council, New York City, 20 July 1992.

51. Lucille Mathurin Mair, "Creative Women in Changing Societies" (speech delivered at the seminar Creative Women in Changing Societies, Oslo, Norway, 1980).

52. Mair, *Historical Study*, 318, 319.

53. Ibid., 326.

54. Lucille Mathurin Mair, speech delivered at the luncheon for Winnie Mandela, Kingston, Jamaica, March 1991.

55. Lucille Mathurin Mair, speech delivered at a meeting of the Business and Professional Women's Club of Jamaica, Kingston, 21 January 1974.

56. Ibid.

57. Lucille Mathurin Mair, "A New Deal for Jamaican Women" (lecture delivered on International Human Rights Day, Kingston, Jamaica, 10 December 1974).

58. Ibid.

59. Lucille Mathurin Mair, speech delivered at the Social Committee the UN Economic and Social Council, New York City, 23 April 1981.

60. Lucille Mathurin Mair, "Creative Women in Changing Societies" (speech delivered at the seminar Creative Women in Changing Societies, Oslo, Norway, 1980).

61. Ibid.

62. Lucille Mathurin Mair, Michael Manley Lecture Series, London, n.d.

63. Lucille Mathurin Mair, speech delivered 11 February 1973.

64. Mair, *Historical Study*, 53.

65. Lucille Mathurin Mair, speech delivered at the opening of the exhibition *Explorations in Clay and Bronze*, National Gallery of Jamaica, Kingston, 1988.

66. Lucille Mathurin Mair, speech delivered on the occasion of the International Day of Peace, Jamaica, 17 September 1991.
67. Ibid.
68. Institute for Gender and Development Studies, "Tribute to Lucille Mair", *Gleaner*, 9 January 2009.
69. Adrienne Germain, president of International Women's Health Coalition and former programme officer responsible for women's programmes at the Ford Foundation, the first funder of the Women's Bureau, quoted in Peggy Antrobus's tribute to Mair at her funeral.
70. Lucille Mathurin Mair, speech delivered upon receiving the CARICOM Triennial Award, 1996.
71. Peggy Antrobus, telephone interview by Stephanie Sewell, June 2018.

BIBLIOGRAPHY

Baugh, Edward. *Chancellor, I Present . . .: A Collection of Convocation Citations Given at the University of the West Indies, Mona, 1985–1998.* Kingston: University of the West Indies Press, 1998.

Bolles, A. Lynn. 2010. Review of *A Historical Study of Women in Jamaica, 1655–1844.* New West Indian Guide 84, nos. 1–2 (2010): 125–27.

Frederick, Rhonda. "Genre, Gender and Eric Walrond's Equivocal Transnational Vision". In *Eric Walrond: The Critical Heritage*, edited by Louis J. Parascandola and Carl A. Wade, 100–127. Kingston: University of the West Indies Press, 2012.

Lewis, Rupert. *Walter Rodney's Intellectual and Political Thought.* Kingston: University of the West Indies Press, 1998.

Mair, Lucille Mathurin. "The Arrival of the Black Woman". *Jamaica Journal* 9, nos. 2 (1975): 2–7.

———. "Commentary on the Ethics of Induced Abortion from a Feminist Perspective". *International Journal of Gynaecology and Obstetrics* 30, supp. (1989): 57–60.

———. *A Historical Study of Women in Jamaica 1655–1844*, edited by Hilary McD. Beckles and Verene A. Shepherd. Kingston: University of the West Indies Press, 2006.

———. "Jamaican Women and the Quest for Economic Independence". *UNESCO Features*, nos. 676–678 (1975): 11–14.

———. *The Rebel Woman in the British West Indies during Slavery.* Kingston: Institute of Jamaica Publications, 1975; reprinted by the University of the West Indies Press, 2007. (For a comparative look at women and resistance, see Hilary McD. Beckles, *Natural Rebels: A Social History of Enslaved Black Women in Barbados* [New Brunswick, NJ: Rutgers University Press, 1989] and *Centering Woman: Gender Discourses in Caribbean Slave Society* [Kingston: Ian Randle, 1998].)

———. "The Student and the University's Civilising Role". *Caribbean Quarterly* 15, nos. 2–3 (1969): 8–19.

Massiah, Joycelin, Elsa Leo-Rhynie and Barbara Bailey. *The UWI Gender Journey: Recollections and Reflections.* Kingston: University of the West Indies Press, 2016.

Nettleford, Rex. *From the Heart: Eulogies.* Kingston: Office of the Vice-Chancellor, University of the West Indies, 2011.

Parascandola, Louis J., and James Davis. "A West Indian Grows in Brooklyn: The Early American Experiences of Eric Walrond". In *Eric Walrond: The Critical Heritage*, edited by Louis J. Parascandola and Carl A. Wade, 188–201. Kingston: University of the West Indies Press, 2012.

Shepherd, Verene A., ed. *Engendering Caribbean History: Cross-Cultural Perspectives.* Kingston: Ian Randle, 2011.

———, ed. *Women in Caribbean History: The British-Colonised Territories.* Kingston: Ian Randle, 1999.

Stienstra, Deborah. *Women's Movements and International Organizations.* New York: St Martin's Press, 1994.

Wade, Carl A., and Louis J. Parascandola. Introduction to *Eric Walrond: The Critical Heritage*, edited by Louis J. Parascandola and Carl A. Wade, 1–15. Kingston: University of the West Indies Press, 2012.

ACKNOWLEDGEMENTS

I thank all those who helped to make this work a reality, especially Lucille Mathurin Mair's children, Adrian, David and Gail Mathurin, and her niece Jeannette Campbell. I also express my appreciation to Sean Mock Yen and the staff of the University of the West Indies Archives and Nadeen Spence of the university's Mary Seacole Hall for allowing me and my research assistant, Stephanie Sewell, access to Mair's underutilized papers. With this treasure trove of documentation, along with oral history sources, the task of getting access to the philosophy and opinions of this rebel woman was not very difficult. We also thank all others who allowed us to interview them so that we could fill out the missing parts of her life that could not be gleaned from other sources: International Court of Justice judge His Excellency Patrick Robinson; past students and colleagues Elsa Leo-Rhynie, Barbara Bailey, Mervyn Morris, Carl Campbell, Maureen Warner Lewis, Marlene Hamilton and Velma Pollard; and ambassadors Evadne Ruby Coye, Patricia Durrant, Sheila Sealy Monteith, Maria Dembowska and Richard Bernal. Her close friends Peggy Antrobus and Irena Cousins also expressed great willingness and gratitude to be involved in this project. In addition, we benefited from Edward Baugh's 1993 interview with Mair, which helped to fill in many of the gaps, especially about her early life. Other willing participants in

ACKNOWLEDGEMENTS

this project were Sir Hilary Beckles, vice chancellor of the UWI and a historian much admired by Mair; Beverley Anderson Duncan; Marjorie Whylie; Elaine Melbourne; Mavis Gilmour; Sonia Mills; Beverley Phillips; former prime minister of Jamaica P.J. Patterson; and the late ambassador and high commissioner of St Kitts and Nevis to Jamaica, Cedric Harper.

I would also like to express thanks to Kristina Neil and Shafique Sam for their assistance in gathering information on Mair. Above all, I thank my research assistant Stephanie Sewell, who took on this project with passion and zeal and who went beyond the call of duty to ensure that the work was completed. Indeed, I regard her as co-author.